W0179772

ABSCHLUSS-
PRÜFUNGS-
TRAINER

Realschulabschluss
Bayern

 Deine **Audios** findest du auf scook.de/bayern. Dafür gibst du den unten stehenden Zugangscode in die Box ein.

 Deine **interaktiven Übungen** kannst du so freischalten:

1. Melde dich auf scook.de/bayern an. Beim ersten Besuch von scook.de/bayern musst du dich mit einer – nicht notwendig personifizierten – E-Mailadresse registrieren.
2. Gib den unten stehenden Zugangscode in die Box ein.
3. Damit deine Lernstandsdaten gespeichert werden, müssen du und deine Eltern uns bei der ersten Freischaltung der interaktiven Übungen eine Einwilligung dazu geben. Cornelsen speichert die Antworten deiner durchgeführten Übungen für die Nutzungsdauer der interaktiven Übungen. Für Volljährige (über 18 Jahren) ist das Einverständnis der Eltern nicht erforderlich.

Die Nutzungsdauer für die Online-Übungen beträgt nach Aktivierung des Zugangscodes zwei Jahre. In dieser Zeit speichern wir deine Lernstandsdaten für dich; nach Ablauf der Nutzungsdauer werden sie gelöscht.

Dein Zugangscode auf
www.scook.de/bayern
azoa6-h24hd

Abschlussprüfungstrainer Englisch

Realschulabschluss | Bayern

Illustrationen
Karen Donnelly, Cornelsen (S. 50; S. 54; S. 57; S. 58; S. 59; S. 60)

Fotos
action press (S. 21: Exclusive Pix) **mauritius images** (S. 18: alamy stock photo/Photo 12; S. 23: alamy stock photo/Penny Tweedie) **Shutterstock** (S. 8: riekephotos; S. 9: oliveromg; S. 10: grynold; S. 11 Freundinnen: Iakov Filimonov, Tiere: Eric Isselee; S. 12 oben: Marsan, unten: Petrenko Andriy; S. 13 Gespräch: Antonio Guillem, Ikon Bücherei und Kino: Alex Oakenman, Ikon Park, Swimming Pool, Zug und Stadium: chartcameraman; S. 15: RossHelen; S. 19: David Pickett; S. 20: Mikhail Kolesnikov; S. 25: Tukaram.Karve; S. 26 oben: szefei, Mitte: Mark LaMoyne, unten: ESB Professional; S. 28: Evocation Images; S. 29: Boyloso; S. 31: Photomika-com; S. 35: mubus7; S. 40: pcruciatti; S. 56: Ociacia; S. 62: Dragan Jovanovic; S. 64: Monkey Business Images; S. 73: Joe Gough; S. 74: Nolte Lourens; S. 76: WitR; S. 82: Billy Stock; S. 83: Constantin Stanciu)

Erarbeitet von: Gwen Berwick, York; Sydney Thorne, York
In Zusammenarbeit mit der Englischredaktion: Klaus Unger (Projektleitung); Cornelia Frisse (verantwortliche Redakteurin)
Beratende Mitwirkung: Sandra Finnegan, Aschaffenburg
Layout-Konzept: Klein&Halm Grafikdesign, Berlin
Umschlaggestaltung: Agentur Rosendahl, Berlin
Layout und technische Umsetzung: Klein&Halm Grafikdesign, Berlin

www.cornelsen.de

Soweit in diesem Lehrwerk Personen fotografisch abgebildet sind und ihnen von der Redaktion fiktive Namen, Berufe, Dialoge und Ähnliches zugeordnet oder diese Personen in bestimmte Kontexte gesetzt werden, dienen diese Zuordnungen und Darstellungen ausschließlich der Veranschaulichung und dem besseren Verständnis des Inhalts.

1. Auflage, 1. Druck 2018

Druck: H. Heenemann, Berlin

ISBN 978-3-06-034861-9

PEFC zertifiziert
Dieses Produkt stammt aus nachhaltig bewirtschafteten Wäldern und kontrollierten Quellen.
www.pefc.de

PEFC/04-31-1156

Inhaltsverzeichnis

Vorwort

TRAINING SECTION

Speaking Test

Listening Test

Written Test, Part I: Reading

Written Test, Part II: Use of English

Written Test, Part III: Guided Writing

MUSTERPRÜFUNGEN

LÖSUNGEN (als Einleger in der Mitte des Heftes)

Was erwartet dich in der Prüfung?

Die Abschlussprüfung an Realschulen in Bayern wird im Fach Englisch zeitlich versetzt durchgeführt:

- Die **mündliche Prüfung** *(Speaking Test)* findet in der letzten Woche vor den Osterferien statt. Die Aufgaben werden vom Kultusministerium gestellt. Geprüft werden zwei (seltener drei) Schüler zusammen durch eine Lehrkraft deiner Schule.

- Die **restliche Prüfung** *(Written Test, Listening Test)* wird zentral vom Kultusministerium entworfen und findet in der Regel im Juni statt.

Die Prüfung ist folgendermaßen aufgebaut:

Kompetenz	Aufgaben	Zeit	Punkte
Speaking Test Sprechfertigkeit	drei Aufgaben: · allgemeine Unterhaltung *(General conversation)* · ein Bild beschreiben und über das dargestellte Thema sprechen *(Responding to visual prompts)* · über eine vorgegebene Situation diskutieren *(Simulated situation)*	12–15 Minuten	30
Listening Test Hörverstehen	fünf Höraufgaben, verschiedene Formate: · Zuordnungsaufgaben *(Matching)* · Auswahlaufgaben *(Multiple choice)* · Lautdiskriminierung *(Error spotting)* · Notizen vervollständigen *(Note taking)* · Satzanfänge ergänzen *(Sentence completion)*	30 Minuten	30
Written Test			
I: Reading Leseverstehen	vier bis fünf Aufgaben, verschiedene Formate: · Richtig/Falsch-Aufgaben *(True, false, not in the text?)* · Zuordnungsaufgaben *(Matching)* · Fehler finden *(Error spotting)* · in die richtige Reihenfolge bringen *(Sequencing)* · Sprachmittlung *(Mediation)* Englisch → Deutsch	105 Minuten	30
II: Use of English Wortschatz, Grammatik	fünf Aufgaben, verschiedene Formate: · Synonyme finden · Wörtern die richtige Bedeutung zuordnen *(Matching)* · die richtige Form eines vorgegebenen Wortes bilden *(Word formation)* · Sätze umformulieren *(Key word transformation)* · Lücken mit Wörtern in korrekter Form füllen *(Fill in the gaps)*		30
III: Guided Writing Schreiben	zwei gelenkte Aufgaben zur Auswahl (E-Mail, Bewerbung, Blog-Eintrag, Story, Artikel etc., 200 Wörter)		30
			150

Themen, Texte und Hilfsmittel in der Prüfung

In der Prüfung wird nicht dein Wissen über ein Thema oder ein Land abgefragt, sondern du sollst zeigen, dass du auf Englisch angemessen und korrekt kommunizieren kannst. Die Themen sind allgemein gehalten, z.B. Umwelt, Verkehr, Technik, Medien, berühmte Persönlichkeiten etc.

Alle Textsorten, denen du in der Prüfung begegnest, dürften dir aus deinem Englischunterricht vertraut sein (Sachtext, Artikel, Romanauszug etc.). Hilfsmittel wie Wörterbücher oder Smartphones sind nicht erlaubt.

Wie arbeitest du mit diesem Heft?

In diesem Heft lernst du durch gezielte Übungen, wie du die Aufgaben zu allen Teilen der Prüfung bearbeiten kannst. Darüber hinaus bekommst du konkrete Prüfungsbeispiele. Das Heft ist deshalb wie folgt aufgebaut:

Das **erste Kapitel**, die *Training Section*, gliedert sich in die fünf Kompetenzbereiche der Prüfung: Sprechfertigkeit, Hörverstehen, Leseverstehen, Wortschatz und Grammatik sowie Schreiben.

Die *Training Section* enthält:
- Hinweise zum Ablauf und zur Bewertung jedes einzelnen Kompetenzbereichs
- Beispiele und Tipps für die häufigsten Aufgabenformate, die dir in der Prüfung begegnen, also *Multiple choice*, *Matching* etc.
- Strategien zum Umgang mit typischen Schwierigkeiten, wie z. B. Verständnisproblemen

> **Tipp**
>
> Blau umrandete Felder markieren Tipps, die dir bei den Aufgaben helfen.

Es empfiehlt sich, die *Training Section* als erstes durchzuarbeiten, und zwar Kompetenzbereich für Kompetenzbereich. So verschaffst du dir einen Überblick darüber, was du schon gut kannst, wo du noch üben solltest und welche Strategien dir dabei helfen.

Das zweite Kapitel bietet dir zwei komplette **Musterprüfungen** *(Written Test, Listening Test)*. Sie sind den Prüfungen der letzten Jahre nachempfunden. Du lernst dadurch Schritt für Schritt die gesamte Prüfungssituation und den Aufbau der Prüfung kennen.

Wenn du feststellst, dass du mit einem Kompetenzbereich oder einem Aufgabenformat noch Schwierigkeiten hast, gehe zurück in die *Training Section* und wiederhole gezielt die entsprechenden Übungen und Strategien oder nutze die Online-Übungen zu Grammatik und Wortschatz auf www.scook.de/bayern.

Die **Tonaufnahmen und Hörtexte** für die *Training Section* und die Musterprüfungen findest du ebenfalls online unter www.scook.de/bayern. Das Kopfhörer-Symbol mit Track-Nummer im Heft zeigt dir an, welchen Hörtext du für die Aufgabe anhören musst.

Anhand der **Lösungen** in der Mitte des Heftes kannst du deine Ergebnisse überprüfen und, wenn nötig, verbessern.

Nützliche **Tipps zur Prüfungsvorbereitung** erhältst du auf Seite 42.

Nun kannst du zuversichtlich sein, dass du weißt, was in der Abschlussprüfung an der Realschule in Bayern auf dich zukommt, und dass du die unterschiedlichen Aufgabenstellungen geübt hast und kennst.

Zusätzlich kannst du dein Grundwissen in den Bereichen Grammatik und Wortschatz mithilfe von Online-Übungen wiederholen und vertiefen. Nutze dazu den Zugangscode auf Seite 1 (www.scook.de/bayern).

Ebenfalls online findest du die Tonaufnahmen zu den Höraufgaben als MP3-Downloads und die dazugehörigen Hörtexte. Nutze dazu ebenfalls den Code von Seite 1.

Viel Spaß beim Training mit diesem Heft und viel Erfolg bei der Prüfung!

Speaking Test

Im Folgenden geht es um die Überprüfung der Sprechfertigkeit im Englischen kurz vor den Osterferien. Sie sollte nicht mit der zusätzlichen mündlichen Prüfung zur Festlegung der Gesamtnote verwechselt werden, die nach den schriftlichen Prüfungen abgelegt werden kann.

> **Tipp**
>
> Du findest zahlreiche Beispielprüfungen im Internet unter www.isb.bayern.de. Gib dort in das Suchfeld **Speaking Realschule** ein und klicke anschließend auf **Weiterentwicklung der Abschlussprüfung Englisch**.

1. Ablauf und Bewertung

Der *Speaking Test* ist eine Partnerprüfung mit je zwei Schülern oder Schülerinnen einer Klasse. Die Zweiergruppen werden gelost und am Prüfungstag bekannt gegeben. Bei einer ungeraden Klassenstärke besteht eine Prüfungsgruppe aus drei Prüflingen. Die Prüfung dauert ungefähr 12 bis 15 Minuten und besteht aus drei Teilen (Parts).

Part 1: Allgemeine Unterhaltung (ca. drei Minuten)

Zum Einstieg tauschst du mit deinem Partner oder deiner Partnerin wichtige Informationen zu deiner Person und deinem persönlichen Umfeld aus, z.B. Familie, Heimatstadt, Hobbys, Freunde, Schule oder Zukunftspläne. Dabei sollst du auch etwas buchstabieren, z.B. einen Namen oder Straßennamen.

Part 2: Ein Bild beschreiben und über das dargestellte Thema sprechen (ca. fünf Minuten)

Ihr erhaltet beide ein Foto und sollt es jeweils etwa eine Minute lang beschreiben bzw. interpretieren. Ausgehend von den auf den Fotos dargestellten Themen tauscht ihr euch anschließend darüber aus, welche Bedeutung das Thema für euch hat.

> **Tipp**
>
> Solltest du etwas nicht verstehen, zögere nicht, auf Englisch nachzufragen:
>
> *Sorry, I didn't understand what you said.*
>
> *Sorry, could you repeat that, please?*
>
> Es ist wichtig, dass du alle Fragen richtig verstehst und dass keine zu langen Gesprächspausen entstehen.

Part 3: Über eine vorgegebene Situation diskutieren (ca. vier Minuten)

Euch wird eine Situation vorgegeben, z.B. die Planung einer Reise. Ihr tauscht eure Gedanken und Vorschläge aus, diskutiert, wägt Argumente ab und versucht, zu einer Problemlösung zu kommen.

Der *Speaking Test* ist Teil der Abschlussprüfung, d.h. du kannst keine gesonderte Note erzielen, sondern sammelst die ersten Punkte für die Gesamtprüfung im Fach Englisch. Maximal kannst du hier 30 der insgesamt 150 Punkte erzielen. Deine Leistung wird anhand von vier Kriterien bewertet:

Kommunikative Kompetenz	Aussprache	Grammatik und Wortschatz	Gesprächsführung
Du ergreifst die Initiative. Du hältst das Gespräch aufrecht und beziehst deinen Partner immer wieder mit ein. Du stellst deiner Partnerin Fragen und gehst auf ihre Redebeiträge ein. Du führst das Gespräch zu einem Ende.	Deine Aussprache und Betonung sind so gut, dass man dich problemlos versteht. Du sprichst flüssig und mit einer natürlichen Satzmelodie.	Du verwendest grammatische Strukturen weitgehend sicher. Einzelne Fehler beeinträchtigen die Kommunikation nicht. Du verfügst über einen breiten Wortschatz, der es dir ermöglicht, über verschiedene Themen differenziert zu sprechen.	Deine Beiträge sind sinnvoll, begründet und angemessen. Deine Gedanken sind klar strukturiert. Du sprichst zum Thema. Du sprichst zusammenhängend und mit der nötigen Länge.

2. Typische Aufgabenformate

In diesem Kapitel lernst du die typischen Aufgabenformate kennen, die dich beim *Speaking Test* an der Realschule in Bayern erwarten. Da es sich um eine Partnerprüfung handelt, ist es sinnvoll, dich zusammen mit einem Freund oder einer Freundin vorzubereiten. Die Tipp-Kästen enthalten nützliche Strategien.

Part 1: Allgemeine Unterhaltung

Im ersten Teil der Prüfung unterhaltet ihr euch so, als ob ihr euch zum ersten Mal begegnet und neugierig aufeinander seid. Es geht nicht nur darum, Fragen zu stellen und zu beantworten, sondern ihr solltet auch aufeinander reagieren und Rückfragen stellen – so wirkt das Gespräch natürlicher.

Der Prüfer oder die Prüferin wird zu euch sagen:

> *I'd like you to pretend that you don't know each other. Ask questions to find out as much information as possible about each other.*

Tipp

Vor der Prüfung:

Wiederhole das **Buchstabieren** auf Englisch (A/R, E/I, G/J...). Welcher Name ist z.B. ESS-OH-PEE-AITCH-EYE-EE?

Bereite **Mindmaps** zu typischen Smalltalk-Themen wie Hobbys, Familie etc. vor.

Wiederhole die **Fragebildung** und bereite einige Fragen vor:
Have you ever ...? When did you first ...? How long have you been ...? Do you often ...?

Ihr könntet euch gegenseitig fragen:

> *Hello. What's your name?*

> *Hi! My name is Nayla. And what's your name?*

> *My name is Felix. How do you spell your name? I've never heard it before.*

> *It's a name from Hawaii. It's spelled N-A-Y-L-A. How are you today, Felix?*

> *I'm fine, thanks. But I feel a bit nervous. What about you?*

> *... So where do you live?*

> *... What are your favourite books/films/subjects/activities/...?*

Tipp

Während der Prüfung:

Euer Gespräch soll möglichst natürlich klingen! Antworte nicht einsilbig, stelle Rückfragen:

How are you today?

Antworte ...
nicht: *Fine. / Bad.*
sondern: *I'm fine, thanks. But I feel a bit nervous. What about you?*

Do you have any brothers or sisters?

Antworte ...
nicht: *Yes. / No.*
sondern: *Yes, I do. My sister is ten and ...*

No, I don't. I'm an only child, and that's the way I like it.

Wende dich deinem Gesprächspartner zu und halte immer Blickkontakt!

Part 2: Ein Bild beschreiben und über das dargestellte Thema sprechen

Hier bekommt ihr beide jeweils ein Farbfoto zur Beschreibung und Interpretation vorgelegt. Du sprichst ca. eine Minute lang über dein Bild und hörst dann zu, während deine Partnerin oder dein Partner über ihr oder sein Bild spricht (oder umgekehrt). Eure beiden Fotos stehen in einem thematischen Zusammenhang, der für das anschließende Gespräch wichtig ist.

Der Prüfer oder die Prüferin sagt:

> *I'm going to give each of you a photograph.*
>
> *Candidate A, here is your photograph. Would you show it to candidate B and talk about it, please?*
>
> *Candidate B, you just listen to candidate A. I'll give you your photograph in a moment.*
>
> *Candidate A, please tell us what you can see in your photograph.*

Tipp

Beim Beschreiben von Bildern kannst du so vorgehen:

1. Sag etwas über das allgemeine Thema des Bildes *(topic sentence)*:
This picture shows two kids on holiday.
In this picture, two kids are on holiday.
(Achtung! *On the picture ...* ist falsch!)

2. Beschreibe das Bild genauer:
I can see a red canoe at the centre of the picture. There are hills in the background.

3. Sage, was die Personen gerade tun. Verwende dafür das *present progressive*:
The girl at the back of the canoe is looking at a map.

4. Spekuliere darüber, was die Personen getan haben oder tun werden:
I think the kids will soon go back home because the weather might change.

5. Sage deine Meinung zum Thema des Bildes:
I like adventure holidays, but I don't like canoeing. I prefer more exciting sports like climbing or abseiling.

Foto A

Tipp

Zum Üben:

Um ein Gefühl für die Länge deiner Bildbeschreibung zu bekommen, kannst du einfach Bilder aus einer Zeitschrift beschreiben und dir dabei eine Stoppuhr auf eine Minute stellen.

Tipp

Was tun, wenn dir ein englisches Wort nicht einfällt? Gib nicht gleich auf!

- Du kannst das Wort vielleicht umschreiben (Foto A):

  The kids are wearing ... clothes filled with air to help them swim. (→ life jackets)

  They are using ... you know ... sticks to move the canoe forwards. (→ paddles)

- Wenn dir das Gegenteil einfällt, kannst du es verneinen (Foto A):

  It is very ... it isn't noisy at all. (→ quiet, peaceful)

- Oder du verwendest ein Wort mit ähnlicher Bedeutung (Foto B):

  The boy is trying to ... get/catch/hit the ball. (→ dig)

  Der Prüferin wird auf diese Weise nicht auffallen, dass du das Wort für Baggern (Volleyball) nicht wusstest.

Anschließend sagt die Prüferin oder der Prüfer:

Now, candidate B, here is your picture. Would you show it to candidate A and tell her/him about it, please?

Tipp

Wiederhole die Ortsangaben zur Bildbeschreibung:

In the foreground/background I can see ...

On the left/right there is/are ...

At the bottom/top/centre ...

In the top left/right corner ...

In the left/right bottom corner ...

There is/are ... next to ... / behind ... / in front of ... / opposite ... / between ...

Tipp

Bereite vor der Prüfung Wortschatz zur Personen-beschreibung vor, z.B.:

clothes: *shorts, sweater, skirt, cardigan, ...*

hair: *long, short, blonde, curly, straight, ...*

appearance: *old, middle-aged, young, handsome, ...*

Foto B

Zum Abschluss von Part 2 fordert die Prüferin oder der Prüfer euch auf, euch über das, was auf euren Bildern dargestellt ist, auszutauschen:

Your photos show young people on holiday. Now I'd like you to talk together about what kind of holidays you like and what kind of holidays you don't like. Explain why and discuss your opinions.

Tipp

Ergreife die Initiative:
Shall I go first?

Höre deiner Partnerin zu und halte Blickkontakt. Frage nach, wenn du etwas nicht verstanden hast:
Could you say that again, please?
Sorry, what did you say?

Nimm Bezug auf das, was dein Partner sagt:
Yes, I agree that canoeing is very relaxing, but ...
That's a good point, but ...
That's true. I once went on an adventure trip and ...

Stelle interessierte Rückfragen:
What do you think about ...?
So what's your favourite ...?
Do you prefer ... or ...?
Why do/don't you like ...?

Bringe deine eigenen Erfahrungen ein:
A few years ago I went to Spain with my parents and ...
I've never played beach volleyball before, but I imagine ...

Gewinne Zeit zum Nachdenken:
That isn't easy to say. Let me think ...
Hang on a second ...
My favourite sort of holiday? Well ...

Part 3: Über eine vorgegebene Situation diskutieren

Euch wird eine Situation geschildert, über die ihr diskutieren sollt. Als Anregung erhaltet ihr auch einige Bilder. Wichtig ist, dass ihr dabei nicht mit der Prüferin oder dem Prüfer redet, sondern miteinander – schaut euch also dabei an und nehmt aufeinander Bezug. Der Prüfer oder die Prüferin sagt:

I'm going to describe a situation to you: you share a flat with a friend and you want to buy a pet together. Talk about different pets. Then decide which one to choose. Explain why and discuss your opinions. Here is a picture with some ideas to help you.

Tipp

Du bekommst Punkte dafür, dass du das Gespräch aufrechterhältst.

Wäge deine Argumente ab und begründe sie, z. B.:
Dogs are good pets because ...

Greife auf Beispiele zurück, z. B.:
Rats can be really good pets. That's surprising, isn't it? But I have a friend who has a rat, and ...

Reagiere auf das, was dein Gegenüber sagt, z. B.:
A snake? Really? Are you serious? Tell me more!

Prüfe, ob ihr zu einem gemeinsamen Ergebnis kommen könnt:
OK, so what have we agreed on so far? Do we prefer ...?
On the one hand ..., on the other hand ...
I know I first argued for ..., but I've changed my mind. Let's agree on ... instead. OK?

Jetzt bist du dran!

Part 1: Allgemeine Unterhaltung

a) Bereite mindestens sechs Fragen vor, durch die du etwas über deine Partnerin oder deinen Partner erfährst:

- drei Fragen mit einem Fragewort *(When/Where/Why/How/What …?)*

_____

_____

_____

- drei Entscheidungsfragen (Fragen, die man mit ja oder nein beantworten kann):

_____

_____

_____

b) Beantworte sechs Fragen deines Partners oder deiner Partnerin. Denk daran: Sei nicht einsilbig!

> How do you spell your name?

> How do you get to school every day?

> How old are you?

> What are your plans for the future?

> What are your favourite subjects at school?

> Where do you live?

> Do you enjoy living in your town? Why (not)?

> Have you ever been to an English-speaking country?

> What's your dream holiday like?

> Do you have any brothers or sisters?

> Which languages do you speak?

Part 2: Ein Bild beschreiben und über das dargestellte Thema sprechen

a) Stell dir eine Stoppuhr auf eine Minute.

b) Beschreibe das erste Bild anhand der fünf Schritte in der Tipp-Box auf Seite 8.

Tipp

Zum Üben: Beschreibt euch gegenseitig einige Bilder.

- Baut bei der Beschreibung inhaltliche Fehler ein und der Partner oder die Partnerin muss die Fehler finden.
- Der Partner oder die Partnerin zeichnet das Bild nach deiner Beschreibung (oder umgekehrt).

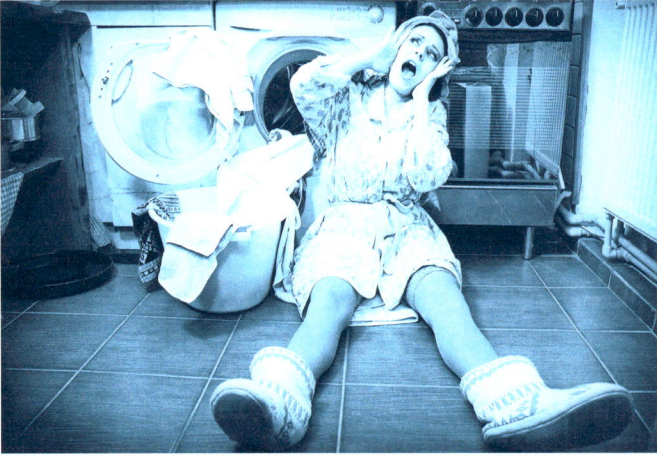

c) Stell dir eine Stoppuhr auf eine Minute und beschreibe das zweite Bild.

Falls du mit einer Partnerin oder einem Partner übst, hörst du nun zu und misst die Zeit.

d) Sprich nun zum Thema Hausarbeit – allein oder (noch besser!) mit einem Partner oder einer Partnerin. Dafür sind drei Minuten Zeit.

> *The photographs show people doing household chores. Now I'd like you to talk about chores that you like or dislike. Explain why and discuss your opinions.*

Part 3: Über eine vorgegebene Situation diskutieren

> *I'm going to describe a situation to you: There's a new student in your class. Your teacher asked you to show the student around your town. Talk about what places your will show him or her. Decide together which three places you are going to go to and where to go first. Explain why and discuss your opinions.*

Tipp

Zum Üben:

Notiere dir wichtige Redemittel zur Meinungsäußerung auf Karteikarten, z.B. aus dem Tipp-Kasten auf S. 11. Ziehe fünf Karten und versuche, diese Redemittel in einer Diskussion unterzubringen. Am besten geht dies mit einem Partner oder einer Partnerin.

a) Stelle eine Stoppuhr auf eine Minute. Überlege, welche drei Orte in deinem Ort für junge Leute wichtig sind. Notiere für jeden der drei Orte ein bis zwei Argumente. Falls du mit einem Partner oder einer Partnerin übst, tut er bzw. sie das gleiche.

Tipp

Achtung! In der Prüfung hast du in der Regel nur wenige Sekunden Zeit zum Überlegen. Übe mit anderen Themen und gib dir selbst immer weniger Zeit zum Nachdenken. Kurz vor der Prüfung solltest du in der Lage sein, dir spontan eine Meinung zu bilden.

---

b) Stellt euch nun eine Stoppuhr auf drei Minuten, diskutiert und einigt euch gemäß Aufgabenstellung.

Listening Test (Hörverstehen)

1. Ablauf und Bewertung

Die Überprüfung des Hörverstehens dauert 30 Minuten. Bei jeder Aufgabe hast du zunächst Zeit, um die Aufgabe zu lesen. Dann hörst du den Hörtext zum ersten Mal und bearbeitest die Aufgabe. Anschließend hörst du den Hörtext noch ein zweites Mal und erhältst Zeit, um deine Antworten zu ergänzen und zu überprüfen. Dies ist das Vorgehen bei allen fünf Aufgaben in der Prüfung.

In den letzten Jahren bestand der *Listening Test* aus den folgenden fünf Aufgabenformaten:

*   *Matching:* Bei der ersten Höraufgabe hörst du einige kurze Hörtexte (Ansagen, Statements etc.) und ordnest sie einer Auswahl an vorgegebenen Themen, Oberbegriffen, Personen etc. zu. Es geht bei dieser Aufgabe nicht um Details, sondern darum, dass du die Hörtexte im Großen und Ganzen („global") verstehst.

*   *Multiple choice:* Bei der zweiten Aufgabe hörst einen Hörtext (meist ein Gespräch mit zwei Sprechern) und erhältst Satzanfänge sowie vier Möglichkeiten, den Satz zu beenden. Du musst die korrekte Fortsetzung durch Ankreuzen auswählen. Dazu solltest du auf die Details achten.

*   *Error spotting:* Bei der dritten Aufgabe hörst du einen Hörtext und kannst ihn gleichzeitig mitlesen. Allerdings sind im Lesetext Fehler versteckt, die du heraushören und unterstreichen musst. Dabei geht es nicht um Grammatik- oder Rechtschreibfehler, sondern um andere Wörter, die ähnlich klingen.

*   *Note taking:* Bei der vierten Aufgabe hörst du einen Hörtext (meist ein Gespräch mit zwei Sprechern) und ergänzt vorgegebene Notizen stichwortartig. Details wie beispielsweise Zahlen, Namen oder Orte sind dabei wichtig.

*   *Note taking / Sentence completion:* Bei der fünften Aufgabe entnimmst du einem Hörtext (meist ein Gespräch mit drei Sprechern) gezielt Informationen. Anschließend ergänzt du vorgegebene Satzanfänge (seltener auch vorgegebene Notizen) in deinen eigenen Worten.

Zwischenfragen an die Lehrkraft, Wörterbücher oder Handys sind nicht erlaubt. Grammatik- oder Rechtschreibfehler werden beim Hörverstehen aber nicht bewertet, solange man deine Antworten noch verstehen kann.

Beim *Listening Test* kannst du 30 Punkte erreichen. Er macht also 20% der Gesamtnote aus.

2. Typische Aufgabenformate

In diesem Kapitel lernst du die typischen Aufgabenformate kennen, die dich bei der Abschlussprüfung an Realschulen in Bayern im Bereich Hörverstehen erwarten.

Beachte: Die Hörtexte in der *Training Section* dienen als Beispiele für bestimmte Aufgabenformate. Sie sind daher teilweise etwas kürzer als in der Prüfung. Längere Hörtexte findest du bei den Musterprüfungen.

Die Tipp-Kästen enthalten nützliche Strategien, wie du mit häufigen Schwierigkeiten umgehen kannst.

Matching: *Radio ads*

Bei der **ersten Höraufgabe** hörst du meist **fünf** kurze Hörtexte (Ansagen, Werbespots, Statements ...). Du musst jeden Hörtext einer von (in der Regel) **acht** vorgegebenen Kategorien (Personen, Themen, Orten ...) zuordnen. Drei Kategorien bleiben also übrig. Es geht bei dieser Aufgabe um dein Globalverstehen, also deine Fähigkeit, den Inhalt im Großen und Ganzen zu erfassen. Die Details sind nicht so wichtig.

Vorgehen in der Prüfung:
- Du hörst eine Einweisung.
- Du erhältst Zeit, die Arbeitsanweisung zu lesen.
- Nach einem Signal hörst du alle fünf Hörtexte mit kurzen Pausen hintereinander und löst die Aufgabe.
- Nach einer kurzen Pause hörst du alle fünf Hörtexte ein zweites Mal.

Hier in der *Training Section* ist die Aufgabe gekürzt: Du hörst **vier** Hörtexte und ordnest sie **sechs** Kategorien A–F zu.

> **Tipp**
>
> Lies alle Kategorien (hier **A–F**) genau durch, bevor du die Hörtexte hörst.
>
> - Im Hörtext kommen wahrscheinlich Wörter vor, die du nicht kennst. Keine Panik! Du kannst diese Aufgabe lösen, ohne dass du alle Wörter im Hörtext verstehst.
> - Du wirst die Formulierungen der Kategorien wahrscheinlich nicht wörtlich hören. Es geht vielmehr darum, dass du den Sinn und den Inhalt des gesamten Hörtextes erfasst.
>
> Beispiel: Im ersten Hörtext wirst du Wörter aus dem Bereich Essen hören: *chicken*, *tomatoes*, *mushrooms* etc. Das **könnte** auf Kategorie **A** hindeuten. **Aber:**
>
> Es ist gefährlich, nur aus Einzelwörtern auf eine Lösung zu schließen! Überlege stattdessen: Worum geht es in diesem Hörtext eigentlich? Was ist die Gesamtsituation? Passt das immer noch zu Kategorie **A**?

You will hear four radio ads. What is the message of each advert? **Write the correct numbers (1–4) in the boxes next to the categories (A–F).** Be careful: Use each number only once.
(You will have 5 seconds after the first listening and 5 seconds after the second listening.)

A Eat healthily	**D** Stay active	
B Work in an old people's home	**E** Advice for owners of birds	
C Buy ethical cosmetics	**F** Recycle	

Multiple choice: *A visit to Krakow*

Bei der **zweiten Höraufgabe** hörst du einen längeren Hörtext, in der Regel ein Gespräch mit zwei Sprechern. Anschließend erhältst du einige (meist vier) Satzanfänge und musst entscheiden, welches der vorgegebenen Satzenden am besten passt. Es gibt in der Regel vier Möglichkeiten (A–D) zur Auswahl, und normalerweise gibt es nur eine richtige Lösung. Wenn mehrere Satzenden richtig sein können, ist das ausdrücklich angegeben.

You will hear an interview with Tim, who has just come back from a visit to Krakow in Poland. One ending to each of the following sentences (1–5) is correct. **Tick (✓) A, B, C or D.**
(You will have 5 seconds after the first listening and 5 seconds after the second listening.)

1 Tim travelled to Krakow ...

A ☐ by train.

B ☐ by plane.

C ☐ by car.

D ☐ by boat and train.

2 In Krakow Tim stayed ...

A ☐ with a family member in a village.

B ☐ with a friend in the town centre.

C ☐ in town, but a little way out of the city centre.

D ☐ in a flat in the city centre.

3 In Krakow Tim visited ...

A ☐ places with few tourists.

B ☐ the main tourist sites.

C ☐ places with no crowds.

D ☐ places with lots going on for tourists.

4 In Krakow Tim made himself understood with English and ...

A ☐ no Polish, but lots of smiles.

B ☐ a little Polish and making signs.

C ☐ Polish that he had learnt at school.

D ☐ fluent Polish.

5 In the future, the main problem for tourists will be that ...

A ☐ the city will be too big.

B ☐ Krakow will be more expensive.

C ☐ they will have to learn Polish.

D ☐ the crowds will be too big.

Tipp

Bei Multiple-choice-Aufgaben hörst du oft nicht genau das gleiche Wort wie in den Antworten **A**, **B**, **C** oder **D**, sondern andere Formulierungen, z.B. in **Satz 1**:

- Statt *by train* hörst du vielleicht *at the station*.
- Statt *by car* hörst du vielleicht *we drove*.
- Statt *by boat* hörst du vielleicht *we took the ferry*.

Welche Formulierung könnte statt *by plane* kommen?

Tipp

Ausschlussverfahren: Wenn du nicht gleich auf die richtige Lösung kommst, überlege, welche Lösungen auf jeden Fall falsch sind. Beispiel:

Satz 2: Du hörst, dass Tim seine Unterkunft im Internet bucht. Welche zwei Lösungen fallen dadurch wohl weg? Nun musst du dich nur noch zwischen zwei Lösungen entscheiden.

Tipp

Vorsicht bei identischen Wörtern in Hörtext und Aufgabe! Sie deuten nicht unbedingt auf die richtige Lösung hin. Beispiel:

Satz 3: Im Hörtext kommt *main tourist sites* vor – wie in Lösung **B**. Ist **B** folglich die richtige Lösung? Nein! Wie könnte das zu erklären sein?

Tipp

Bei Multiple-choice-Aufgaben werden einzelne Wörter aus dem Hörtext oft ersetzt durch:
- **Synonyme** (Wörter und Ausdrücke mit ähnlicher Bedeutung, wie *great – wonderful*)
- **Antonyme** (Wörter und Ausdrücke mit gegensätzlicher Bedeutung, wie *great – awful / not great at all*)

Dieses Wissen kann dir helfen, die richtige Lösung zu finden, z. B. in **Satz 4**:

Synonyme:
a few words of Polish (Hörtext) = *a little Polish* in **B**

use your hands (Hörtext)   = _____ in **B**

Also ist **B** wahrscheinlich die richtige Antwort!

Antonyme:
taught myself (Hörtext)   ≠ *learnt at school* in **C**

a few words of Polish (Hörtext) ≠ _____ in **A**

      und ≠ _____ in **D**

Also scheiden **A**, **C** und **D** wahrscheinlich aus.

Tipp

Satz 5: Vorsicht! **Drei** der vier Probleme **A–D** kommen im Hörtext vor, aber zwei sind Nebenprobleme, die zum Hauptproblem beitragen. Und hier wird nach dem **Haupt**problem gefragt!

Error spotting: *A tourist attraction in Brighton*

Bei der **dritten Höraufgabe** geht es darum, ganz genau hinzuhören. Du hörst einen Text (meist einen Bericht), den du mitlesen kannst. Im Lesetext sind jedoch einige Fehler versteckt, die du finden sollst: Anstelle des im Hörtext gesprochenen Wortes steht dort ein anderes, aber sehr ähnlich klingendes Wort. Bei dieser Aufgabe steht also nicht so sehr das Textverständnis im Vordergrund, sondern deine Fähigkeit, ähnlich klingende Wörter beim Hören zu unterscheiden. Inhalt und Zusammenhang können dir dabei allerdings helfen.

> You will hear a report from a famous tourist site in Brighton. **Underline the wrong words in the text and write the correct version in the space provided.**
> (You will have 10 seconds after the first listening and 15 seconds after the second listening.)

Tipp

Lies zunächst den Lesetext. Es lohnt sich, Vermutungen anzustellen, welche Wörter falsch sein könnten:
* Achte auf Zahlen – sie werden häufig leicht geändert!
* Achte auf Wörter, die dir beim Lesen merkwürdig vorkommen. Beispiel: Im letzten Satz steht *the servants prepared the viewed*. Hier passen die Wortarten nicht so recht zusammen. Höre also an dieser Stelle genau hin!
* Achte auch auf den Unterschied zwischen ähnlich klingenden Konsonanten, z.B. [v] wie in *very* oder *viewed* und [f] wie in *ferry* oder _____ .

Beim ersten Hören kannst du die Wörter einfach unterstreichen. Beim zweiten Hören kannst du dich dann gezielt auf diese Wörter konzentrieren.

Die Punktzahl der Aufgabe gibt dir an, wie viele Fehler du finden musst. Pro Zeile gibt es nur maximal einen Fehler.

The Royal Pavilion in Brighton

Here I am in Brighton, standing outside a strange, exotic-looking building, _____

in a park with exotic trees and plants, with lots of flowers, and five onion- _____

shaped domes that don't look English at all. In fact, this building looks like _____

a palace out of a child's book of fairy tales. Well, it is a palace – a real one. _____

It was built between 1850 and 1822 for the son of the king of England, a _____

prince called George. Prince George did not like walking, and found London _____

too serious – he preferred dancing and thinking and having expensive _____

parties with his friends. So the palace – called the Royal Pavilion – was _____

built to give Prince George a place where he should escape life in "boring" _____

London. _____

Today the palace is open to the public. You can walk through the living _____

rooms, bedrooms, music rooms and dining hall of George and his rich _____

friends, but also through the kitchens where the servants prepared the _____

viewed and did the washing up. It's the contrast between these two _____

lifestyles that makes a visit so special. _____

(6)

Note taking: Bob Marley

Bei der **vierten Höraufgabe** hörst du einen längeren Dialog oder ein Interview. Deine Aufgabe ist es, gezielt bestimmte Informationen aus dem Text herauszuhören und zu notieren. Dies tust du, indem du vorgegebene Notizen (z.B. in einer Tabelle oder in einem Formular) stichwortartig ergänzt.

Radio presenter Joshua Needham is talking to Reggae expert Gwen Devlin about the Jamaican singer-songwriter Bob Marley.
Listen to the interview and **take notes**. You do not have to write complete sentences but **one word is not enough**.
(You will have 10 seconds after the first listening and 20 seconds after the second listening.)

Tipp

- Hier wird von dir häufig verlangt, Zahlen oder Namen zu verstehen und mitzuschreiben (Jahre, Preise, Telefonnummern, Email-Adressen, Websites etc.).

- In Aufgabe **6** kannst du die Antwort in deinen eigenen Worten geben. Du brauchst nicht Wort für Wort aus dem Hörtext zu zitieren.

Bob Marley – the most famous Jamaican ever?		
0 Born in (country):	*in Jamaica*	
1 Born in (month, year):		1
Age of parents at Bob's birth: **2** Mother: **3** Father:		2
4 Name of his first band:		1
5 Name of a famous song:		1
6 Marley was controversial because …	1) 2)	2

Note taking / Sentence completion: *A guided tour of Bo-Kaap*

Die **fünfte Höraufgabe** enthält ein längeres Gespräch oder Interview mit (in der Regel) drei Sprechern. Wieder ist es deine Aufgabe, gezielt bestimmte Informationen aus dem Text herauszuhören und zu notieren. Meist erhältst du dazu Satzanfänge, die du in deinen eigenen Worten ergänzt. Es kann aber auch eine Tabelle oder ein Formular mit fehlenden Informationen vorgegeben sein.

5

A guide is showing tourists around the district of Bo-Kaap in Cape Town, South Africa.
Listen to the guide and the tourists **and take notes.** Be careful, **one word is not enough**.

(You will have 30 seconds after the first listening and 90 seconds after the second listening.)

1   There were Muslims in South Africa in 1794 because ...

_____

_____   1

Tipp
Satz 1: Für die inhaltlich korrekte Antwort gibt es verschiedene Formulierungen oder Schwerpunkte!

2   The number of Asian South Africans today is ...

_____   1

Tipp
Satz 2: Vorsicht! Im Hörtext kommt die Zahl ganz vorn im Satz. Du musst sie dir also merken oder beim ersten Hören notieren:
_____ *Asians live in South Africa.*

3   Outside of Cape Town, Asian workers worked in ...

_____ or _____   1

Tipp
Satz 3: Für den Punkt musst du zwei Informationen wiedergeben!

4   At the Bo-Kaap museum you can see ... _____

_____   1

Tipp
Satz 4: Die Antwort „Möbel" ist richtig, aber du musst ja mehr als ein Wort schreiben. Ergänze also eine weitere relevante Information über diese Möbel.

5   Bo-Kaap has changed in the last few years. For example, ...

_____

and _____   2

Tipp
Satz 5: Beschränke deine Antwort auf das, was sich **geändert** hat. Weitere Details (*colourful houses*, *quiet streets* etc.) sind hier nicht gefragt. Für die zwei Punkte musst du zwei von mehreren möglichen Aspekten nennen!

A street in Bo-Kaap

3. Umgang mit Verständnisproblemen

Die Hörtexte in der Abschlussprüfung enthalten manchmal Wörter, die du vielleicht nicht kennst oder die du nicht verstehst. Das ist ganz normal. Also keine Panik – es gibt Strategien, die dir helfen, die wesentlichen Inhalte trotzdem zu erfassen und die Aufgabe zu lösen. In diesem Kapitel werden anhand der Tonspur eines Werbefilms über die Niagarafälle die wichtigsten Strategien vorgestellt.

Multiple choice: The Niagara Falls (Part 1)

6

You will hear the audio track of a publicity film about the Niagara Falls.
One ending to each of the following sentences (1–2) is correct. **Tick (✓) A, B, C** or **D.**

1 The Horseshoe Falls are …

   A ☐ in Buffalo.

   B ☐ fully in Canada.

   C ☐ for the most part in Canada.

   D ☐ in the USA.

2 The tourists on the *Maid of the Mist* …

   A ☐ protect themselves with a spray.

   B ☐ splash themselves with water.

   C ☐ are wearing raincoats.

   D ☐ take a shower in the waterfalls.

Tipp

Es empfiehlt sich, vor dem ersten Hören immer die Satzanfänge zu lesen!

Tipp

Satz 1: Was kannst du tun, wenn du die entscheidende Stelle beim ersten Hören nicht gut verstanden hast?

Wende das **Ausschlussverfahren** an:
- Was erfährst du über Buffalo? _____
  Antwort **A** scheidet also schon einmal aus.
- Es geht in der Aufgabenstellung um die Horseshoe Falls, nicht die gesamten Niagarafälle. Dadurch scheidet eine weitere Antwort aus, nämlich _____.
- Um dich zwischen den letzten beiden verbliebenen Antworten zu entscheiden, musst du beim zweiten Hören noch einmal ganz genau auf die entscheidende Stelle achten (auf das Keyword Horseshoe Falls):

But these amazing falls, called the Horseshoe Falls, are the biggest and they're _____ in Canada.

Die richtige Antwort ist also _____.

Tipp

Satz 2: Vorsicht! In den Lösungsmöglichkeiten **A–D** kommen Wörter vor, die du aus dem Hörtext erkennst *(spray, splash, shower, …)*. Das heißt aber nicht unbedingt, dass diese Lösungen richtig sind! Aber auch, wenn du die Wörter *spray* und *splash* nicht kennst, kannst du **A** und **B** ausschließen. Wie? Du hörst:
The air is full of spray from the splashing water. Beide Wörter beziehen sich also auf das Wasser, und nicht auf die Touristen.

Error spotting: *The Niagara Falls (Part 2)*

7

> You will hear the second part of the audio track of a publicity film about the Niagara Falls.
> **Underline the wrong words in the text and write the correct version in the space provided.**

Accessing the falls is easy. That's great because it means that thousands

of people can come and see the fantastic light. But it also means that

the falls have to be well protected and taken share of. In fact, these falls

on the American side are actually part of the county's oldest state park.

It was designed by the same man who made out this well-known park ...

Do you recognize it? It's Central Park in New York City. Luckily state parks

don't charge entrance – so you don't have to pay to see the falls. Tourists

can land right next to the top of the Horseshoe Falls and watch the water

spilling over. Isn't it amazing?

_____

_____

_____

_____

_____

_____

_____

_____

_____

Tipp

Lies den Text vor dem ersten Hören und markiere die Wörter, die dir merkwürdig vorkommen! So kannst du beim Hören besser auf diese Stellen achten!

Note taking / Sentence completion: *The Niagara Falls (Part 3)*

8

> You will hear the third part of the audio track of a publicity film about the Niagara Falls. **Listen and take notes.** Be careful, **one word is not enough**.

1 Annie Taylor went over the falls in order to ... _____

_____

2 She asked the first group of friends to ... _____

_____

3 After her experiment, Annie warned ... _____

_____

Tipp

Selbst, wenn du die Textstelle nicht verstanden hast, in der gesagt wird, zu welchem Zweck sich Annie die Niagarafälle hinabstürzte, kannst du Satz **1** ergänzen. Was weißt du nämlich über ihre Lebenssituation?
Auch bei den anderen Satzanfängen helfen dir der gesunde Menschenverstand oder dein Globalverstehen weiter.

Tipp

Du brauchst in der Prüfung natürlich nicht den genauen Wortlaut aufzuschreiben. Im Gegenteil – es ist gut, wenn du deine eigenen Worte verwendest. Oftmals findest du die Antwort sowieso nicht wörtlich im Text, sondern du musst dir deine eigenen Gedanken machen.

Annie Taylor, the first person to survive a trip over the Niagara Falls in a barrel

Written Test, Part I: Reading (Leseverstehen)

Die schriftliche Prüfung *(Written Test)* besteht aus drei Teilen:
* **Part I: Leseverstehen** *(Reading)*
* Part II: Wortschatz und Grammatik *(Use of English)*
* Part III: gelenktes Schreiben *(Guided Writing)*

Für diese drei schriftlichen Prüfungsteile hast du insgesamt 105 Minuten Zeit. Du kannst dir diese Zeit selbst einteilen. Plane also genügend Zeit für jeden Teil ein und bedenke dabei, dass du am Ende auch noch Zeit zum Korrekturlesen benötigst.

1. Ablauf und Bewertung

Im ersten Teil (Part I) der schriftlichen Prüfung liest du meist einen längeren und einige kürzere Texte (Sachtexte, Artikel, Buchauszüge, Werbeanzeigen, Info-Grafiken etc.) und bearbeitest Aufgaben dazu.

Typische Aufgabenformate dafür sind:
* *True, false or not in the text?*
* *Matching*
* *Error spotting*
* *Sequencing (Put into the correct order)*
* *Mediation*

Es empfiehlt sich, den Text zur Aufgabe zunächst einmal komplett zu lesen, um dir einen Überblick über Textsorte und Inhalt zu verschaffen. Anschließend solltest du die Aufgabenstellung gründlich lesen. Nun weißt du, worauf es ankommt, und kannst beim nochmaligen Lesen wichtige Textpassagen markieren.

Im Bereich Leseverstehen musst du wenig selbst schreiben. Falls dies in einigen Aufgaben aber doch der Fall sein sollte, führen Rechtschreib- und Grammatikfehler nicht automatisch zum Punktabzug. Wichtig ist, dass man den Sinn deiner Sätze noch versteht.

Wörterbücher oder andere Hilfsmittel sind nicht erlaubt. Aber zahlreiche Aufgaben kannst du auch lösen, wenn du einige Wörter nicht kennst. Und viele Wörter kannst du dir auch erschließen (Zusammenhang, Ähnlichkeit zu anderen Wörtern etc.).

Beim Leseverstehen kannst du maximal 30 Punkte erreichen. Das macht 20 % der Gesamtnote aus.

2. Typische Aufgabenformate

In diesem Kapitel lernst du die Textsorten und Aufgabenformate kennen, die dich bei der Realschulabschlussprüfung in Bayern im Bereich Leseverstehen am häufigsten erwarten.

Beachte: Die Lesetexte in der *Training Section* dienen als Beispiele für bestimmte Aufgabenformate. Sie sind daher teilweise kürzer als in der Abschlussprüfung. Längere Lesetexte findest du in den Musterprüfungen.

Die Tipp-Kästen enthalten nützliche Strategien, wie du mit typischen Schwierigkeiten umgehen kannst.

Australia's Stolen Generations

The following text is from a museum about Aboriginal people in Australia.

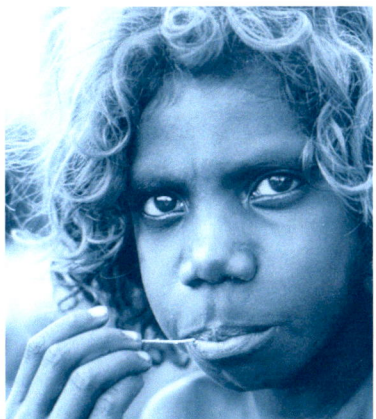

Aboriginal child in Australia

1 In 1915 the government of New South Wales in Australia made a new rule that allowed officials to take Aboriginal children away from their mothers and fathers – even if the parents tried to resist. Other Australian states later did the same.

5 2 This was the fate of over 250,000 Aboriginal children, some say as many as 500,000, who had to leave their homes.

3 The children from Aboriginal families were housed in new English-speaking homes where they were not allowed to speak their own language. And they were given the typical foods of white Australians, even though they weren't used to it.

10 4 The parents were not told where their children were, and the children were not allowed to get in touch with their parents. The result was that the children had no contact with their families, their language, their music and their former way of life.

15

True, false or not in the text?

Bei diesem sehr häufigen Aufgabenformat musst du ganz genau lesen. Meist wird die Information aus dem Text etwas umformuliert und du musst entscheiden, ob die Aussage in Bezug auf den Text noch korrekt ist oder nicht. Oft kommen hier Synonyme (Wörter mit gleicher oder ähnlicher Bedeutung) zum Einsatz.

Tipp

Bei Aufgaben zum Leseverstehen werden Informationen aus dem Text oft in anderen Worten wiedergegeben. Auch Zahlen können auf verschiedene Weise ausgedrückt werden.

Ist die Bedeutung gleich oder ähnlich (Synonyme!), ist die Aussage wahrscheinlich richtig!

Unterscheidet sich die Bedeutung stark, ist die Aussage wahrscheinlich falsch!

Lies die Aufgaben 1 und 2 auf Seite 24 und überprüfe:

	im Text:	in der Aufgabe:	Ist die Bedeutung gleich oder ähnlich?
1	*rule*	*law*	ja / nein
	*... take (...) children **away** from their mothers and fathers*	*... children to be **removed** from their families*	ja / nein
	in 1915	*in the **early 20th century***	ja / nein
2	***250,000** to **500,000***	***more than half a million***	ja / nein
	*from their **mothers** and **fathers***	*from their **parents***	ja / nein

Aber Achtung! Oft sind in einer Aufgabe mehrere Informationen umformuliert – wie hier in Satz 2.
Die Aussage ist nur dann als *true* zu werten, wenn **alle** Informationen eine zumindest ähnliche Bedeutung haben. Was heißt das für Satz 2? Satz 2 ist _____.

Read the text *Australia's Stolen Generations* on page 23. Are sentences 1–4 *True* (T) or *False* (F)? Choose *Not in the text* (N) if there is not enough information to answer *True* or *False*. **Tick (✓) the correct answer**.

		T	F	N
1	The law that allowed Aboriginal children to be removed from their families was introduced in the early 20th century.	☐	☐	☐
2	More than half a million Aboriginal children were taken away from their parents.	☐	☐	☐
3	Fortunately some nicer officials allowed the parents to look for their children.	☐	☐	☐
4	After a few years the Aboriginal Australian children lost touch with their culture.	☐	☐	☐

Tipp

Weitere Möglichkeiten, dieselbe Information etwas anders zu formulieren (Aufgabe **4**):

Ein Sammelbegriff statt einzelner Begriffe:

	im Text:	in der Aufgabe:	Ist die Bedeutung gleich oder ähnlich?
4	*families, language, music, way of life*	_ _ _ _ _ _ _	ja / nein

Synonyme Formulierungen:

	im Text:	in der Aufgabe:	Ist die Bedeutung gleich oder ähnlich?
4	*had no contact with …*	*they* _ _ _ _ _ _ _ _ *with …*	ja / nein

Matching (headings and paragraphs)

Es gibt viele verschiedene Arten von Matching-Aufgaben. In der Prüfung musst du beim Leseverstehen häufig eine Auswahl an Überschriften *(headings)* einzelnen Absätzen *(paragraphs)* zuordnen. Andere Möglichkeiten sind: die Zuordnung von Satzanfängen zu Satzenden, die Zuordnung von Sätzen zu bestimmten Leerstellen im Text, von Personen zu Aussagen, von Ländern zu Informationen etc.

Read the text *Australia's Stolen Generations*. **Match the headings (A–E) with the paragraphs (1–4)** and write the correct numbers in the boxes. Use each number only once. Be careful, there is **one heading** that you do **not need**.

A A different life ☐

B A terrible law ☐

C Families ☐

D Large numbers ☐

E All alone ☐

Tipp

Auch hier helfen dir wieder Synonyme und Sammelbegriffe:

law (Überschrift **B**) = *rule* (Absatz **1**)

large numbers (Überschrift **D**) = 200,000 / 500,000 (Absatz **2**)

Doch Vorsicht bei gleichen Wörtern! Das Wort *families* kommt in Überschrift **C** und in den Absätzen **3** und **4** vor. Aber geht es in diesen beiden Absätzen wirklich um das Familienleben der Kinder? Nein! Eigentlich geht es um das Gegenteil …

Kasun

The following text is from a story about Kasun, a boy in Sri Lanka. In this extract, Kasun writes about his first day at a new school.

On the first day at my new school in Colombo I was scared stiff. Not that I showed it, of course. I pretended to be relaxed. **(1)**
My mum appeared to be calm, but I knew her better. **(2)** Her red eyes told their own story.
When I got to school, all the other kids in Grade 9 seemed to know each other, maybe
5   because they all lived in Colombo. Even the teachers had the same accent as they did.
But I was from Kuruwita, a smaller town outside the capital, and I didn't know anybody. **(3)**
"Hey, what's your name?"
I turned round and saw a big boy. He was smiling. But was he talking to me? **(4)**
I didn't dare answer.
10   "Hey, what's the problem?" said the boy, and took a step closer to me. **(5)**
Was he going to hit me?
"Do you think I'm going to bite you? Hi. I'm Sahan."
"I ... I'm Kasun," I stuttered. "I'm not from Colombo. **(6)** I'm from Kuruwita, but I ..."
"Hey, calm down, you're talking too fast," laughed Sahan.

Matching (removed sentences and gaps)

In diesem Beispiel für eine Matching-Aufgabe sollst du Sätze, die aus einem Lesetext entfernt wurden, den richtigen Stellen (Lücken) im Text zuordnen. Es gibt in der Regel mehr Lücken als Sätze. Dieses Aufgabenformat kam in den vergangenen Jahren häufig zum Einsatz. Um die richtige Lücke im Text zu finden, hilft es, die Sätze vor und nach der Lücke genau zu lesen.

> Look at the extract from *Kasun*. Four sentences have been removed from the text. Choose the correct gap **(1–6)** in the text for each of the sentences below **(A–D)**. **Write the correct number of the gap behind each sentence.** Be careful: There are **two gaps** which you do **not need to use.**

A   I felt like a fish out of water.   ☐

B   But all the time my knees were like jelly.   ☐

C   I couldn't help but see his big hands.   ☐

D   Or to somebody behind me?   ☐

Tipp

Was kann dir hier helfen? Konzentriere dich auf die Sätze vor und nach den Lücken:

- **Synonyme:** Schau im Text nach Formulierungen mit einer ähnlichen Bedeutung, z.B.
  I felt like a fish out of water. (**A**) = *I didn't know anybody.* → Lücke ____

- **Gegensätze:** Das Wort *But ...* in Satz **B** leitet einen Gegensatz ein. Im Satz davor muss also etwas Gegenteiliges stehen: *I pretended to be **relaxed**. But ... my **knees** were **like jelly*** → Lücke ____

- **Kontext:** *... see his big hands.* (**C**) – *Was he going to hit me?* → Lücke ____

My favourite British planes

A However, what had been its big advantage in the 1930s became its big disadvantage ten years later. Taking off from land became faster and easier, while taking off from water was slower and more difficult. And that – unfortunately – meant the end for the flying boats.

B

Flying Today, June Edition

In this edition, three pilots who have flown a number of different planes from different eras tell us about their favourite British planes of all time.

C **Sanjay Gupta, Senior Flight Officer**

My favourite British plane of all time? Well, definitely not the *Comet,* which was responsible for so many deaths. For me the best plane is *Concorde,* of course! OK, it's not strictly only a British plane in that it was designed and built in Britain and France. But what a plane! Its first flight, in 1969, was only 17 years after the *Comet,* yet its technology was light years better! And it flew with practically no accidents for 34 years – till 2003.
What made it radically new, of course, was that it was supersonic: it flew faster than sound! Its top speed was more than twice the speed of sound. In fact, its fastest ever flight from New York JFK to London Heathrow was a record of two hours and 53 minutes. That was in 1996 – and the record still holds today. That's awesome.

D **Carmina Diego, Pilot**

I agree that the *Empire* was a great plane, but my vote would be for the *Comet.* It was built after the Second World War and had its first passenger flight in 1952. What people most remember about the *Comet* today is that it had a number of crashes which nobody could explain. By the time the engineers found out that it was the new technology in the engine that was responsible for the problems, it was too late. The crashes had turned the airlines against the *Comet,* and the number of planes built was disappointingly small.

E But *Concorde* had one big problem that it never overcame. In the time of the jumbo jets, airlines needed bigger and bigger planes, and *Concorde* carried too few passengers to make it attractive to airlines. The result was that the airlines found *Concorde* expensive to run, and that's why *Concorde* was finally taken out of service in 2003.

F **Stuart Jones, Pilot**

My favourite British plane is the *Empire* – called the *Short Empire* because it was built by a company called Short Brothers. It was perfect for its time, which was in the 1930s. Back then many places in the world didn't have airports, and the amazing thing about the *Empire* was that it landed on lakes or on the sea. It didn't have to have a landing strip – just a big area of water would do. That's why they were so often called flying boats. And you could even say that it kept the British Empire together because it flew and carried mail from London to South Africa, Australia or the Caribbean.

G But in my opinion this is unfair. To begin with, the *Comet* was very successful and passengers loved it. And it was a fantastically modern plane for its time. In fact, what makes it so special in the history of flying is that it was the world's very first passenger jet. The only jet planes back then were military planes, so the *Comet* is the grandaddy of all our passenger jets today.

Sequencing (Put into the correct order)

Bei diesem Aufgabenformat gilt es, die Absätze eines Textes in die inhaltlich richtige Reihenfolge zu bringen.

The text on page 26 is from a magazine for flying enthusiasts. The paragraphs of the text are mixed up. **Put the different parts (A–G) into the correct order. Write your answers in the grid below.** One part has already been put in the correct place.

Tipp

Den ersten Teil des Textes erkennst du meist daran, dass er den Inhalt des gesamten Textes einleitet *(topic sentence)*. Das ist hier Textteil ____ .

Bezieht sich eine Textstelle auf eine andere Textstelle? Dann kommt sie in der Reihenfolge weiter hinten.

Beispiel:
Sanjay Gupta (**C**) bezieht sich auf die *Comet*, die schon von Carmina Diego (**D**) erwähnt wurde. Also kommt Textteil **D** in der Reihenfolge weiter vorne. Carmina Diego spricht wiederum von der *Empire*, die zuvor bereits von Stuart Jones (**F**) erwähnt wurde. Also ist Textteil **F** noch weiter vorne.

1	2	3	4	5	6	7
			D			

Matching (statements/questions and objects)

Es können dir auch Matching-Aufgaben begegnen, bei denen du Aussagen oder Fragen zu im Text beschriebenen Personen, Meinungen, Dingen (hier: Flugzeugen) etc. zuordnen musst.

Read the texts about the three planes and **match the planes with the statements 1–6 below.** Choose the correct plane and **write its letter (A, B, C) in the box.** The planes may be chosen more than once. (A: Empire; B: Comet; C: Concorde)

Tipp

Lies den Text Absatz für Absatz. Nach jedem Absatz schaust du dir die Statements **1–6** an und schaust, ob du bereits ein Statement sicher zuordnen kannst. So gibt es von Absatz zu Absatz weniger Statements zur Auswahl, und deine Arbeit wird einfacher.

1 Its main problem was that it could never offer enough seats. ☐

2 It suffered from the fact that there were too many accidents. ☐

3 It had a very good safety record. ☐

4 It made communication between different parts of the British Empire easier. ☐

5 It was a brilliant plane when there weren't the runways and infrastructure that we have today. ☐

6 All modern passenger planes, in a sense, are developed from it. ☐

The Isle of Man TT Race

Error spotting (Write the word which should not be there on the lines …)

Bei diesem Aufgabenformat liest du einen Text, der einige Fehler in Form von überflüssigen Wörtern enthält. Durch diese Wörter wird der jeweilige Satz grammatikalisch falsch oder inhaltlich unlogisch. Deine Aufgabe ist es, diese falschen Wörter zu identifizieren und zu notieren.

> Read the blog about the Isle of Man TT Race and look carefully at each line. Some lines are correct, but **six** of the lines 1–10 have a word which should not be there. **Write the words which should not be there on the lines next to the text.** There is one example **(0)** at the beginning.

Tipp

Lies die Sätze sehr genau. Hier geht es häufig um Grammatik. Schau dir das Beispiel an:
Wie steigert man das kurze Adjektiv *quiet*? *(quieter, quietest)* Nur längere Adjektive steigert man mit *more* und *most*. Das überflüssige Wort ist im ersten Satz also _ _ _ _.

Vorsicht auch bei Wörtern, die zwar oft aufeinander folgen, aber in diesem Text nicht passen, z. B. *have had, because of …*

The Isle of Man is a small island between Britain and Ireland. It is famous for its motorcycle racing. This text is from a blog written by a resident on the Isle of Man.

0	I live on one of Europe's most quietest islands – the Isle of Man. We have beautiful	*most*
1	countryside and narrow country roads, and every May or June we have had the TT	
2	(Tourist Trophy) race.	
3	It's a truly unique race because of it takes place on our public roads. So every year,	
4	the roads that are closed to the public for two weeks. The result is a fortnight of	
5	road chaos on the island, when it's hard for locals to get from the one part of the	
6	island to another.	
7	I am not a motorbike fan and I hate the crowds and the absolute terrible noise. But I	
8	have found a good solution. Every year I book my holidays while the racing takes place.	
9	I wanted sunbathe on a beach in Spain and pay for my holiday by renting out my little	
10	house to TT visitors.	

Tourist Trophy race, Isle of Man (2015)

Filming in New Zealand

This text is taken from an article in a film magazine.

In the past two decades, New Zealand has become home to one of the world's most vibrant film industry. New Zealand's breathtaking landscape has long attracted the world's top film directors. But in recent years New Zealand's high-quality post-production industries such as special effects companies have brought even more international productions to the country.

The *Lord of the Rings* trilogy, for example, was filmed in different areas of New Zealand at the turn of the millennium. Most scenes were shot in the country's national parks, which provided spectacular mountains, a treeless live volcano, and wild, isolated rivers, lakes and canyons. Other scenes were filmed in the softer and less dramatic green hills near Matamata.

One of the advantages of filming in New Zealand is the small number of people living there: only four and half million people in a country more or less the same size as the United Kingdom (population 64 million). So there are fewer buildings, roads and power lines to ruin the views of open countryside.

Another successful fantasy film which was shot and produced in New Zealand is Disney's adventure movie *Pete's Dragon*. It required giant redwood trees, a wild river where a bear could scare the hero, and bare mountains with cliffs from which a dragon could appear. The wonderfully-named Whakarewarewa Forest near Rotorua has Californian redwood trees, the McLaren Falls Park features the wild river and the dramatic Deer Park Heights near Queenstown provided the remote and rugged mountains. And a helicopter company based in Queenstown helped to film the dragon as it flew over the mountains – not the only example of how filming brings employment to more than only actors.

Indeed, many of the visual effects that make the dragon seem so lifelike were created in offices in Wellington, New Zealand's capital and second largest city – which has itself featured in a number of films. In the 2005 remake of the famous film classic *King Kong*, for example, many of the scenes supposedly set in New York were actually filmed in Wellington. This means that the southernmost capital city in the world has its own booming film industry and professional experience of working with some leading film directors in the world.

This volcano was used to represent the place where the Ring was destroyed

Mediation

Bei diesem sehr häufigen Aufgabenformat liest du einen englischen Text und beantwortest dazu Fragen stichpunktartig auf Deutsch. Es geht dabei nicht um eine wortwörtliche Übersetzung, sondern darum, die wesentlichen Informationen wiederzugeben.

> Verwende die Informationen aus dem Artikel über die Filmindustrie in Neuseeland (Seite 29).
> **Bearbeite die Aufgaben (1–6) stichpunktartig auf Deutsch.** Es ist keine wörtliche Übersetzung nötig, die Aspekte müssen **inhaltlich** jedoch **vollständig** erfasst sein. Einzelwörter genügen nicht als Antwort.

Tipp

Lies den ganzen Text. Informationen, die du für deine Antworten brauchst, können aus mehr als nur einem Satz im Text stammen. Markiere sie.

In der Regel sind die Fragen in chronologischer Reihenfolge gestellt. Das heißt, dass du die Informationen zur Beantwortung der ersten Fragen meist am Anfang des Textes findest und die Antworten zu den letzten Fragen eher hinten im Text.

Wichtig: Gib nur das wieder, was im Text steht. Deine sonstigen Kenntnisse sind hier nicht gefragt!
Achte auch im Deutschen auf korrekte Rechtschreibung.

Sei präzise in deinen Antworten: Wenn nur eine Antwort (ein Aspekt) verlangt wird, du aber zwei Antworten gibst, so kann das zu Punktabzug führen.

1 Was zieht internationale Filmemacher nach Neuseeland? **(2 Aspekte)**

_____

_____ **2**

2 In was für Gebieten von Neuseeland wurde *Lord of the Rings* gefilmt? **(2 Aspekte)**

_____

_____ **2**

3 Wie groß ist Neuseeland im Vergleich zu Großbritannien?

_____ **1**

4 Welche Berufsgruppen in Neuseeland profitierten – neben der Filmindustrie selbst – noch von *Pete's Dragon*? **(2 Aspekte)**

_____

_____ **2**

5 Wie half eine Firma aus Queenstown, eine Szene in *Pete's Dragon* zu filmen?

_____ **1**

6 Inwiefern hat die Hauptstadt Neuseelands, Wellington, selbst eine Rolle im Film gespielt?

_____ **1**

3. Umgang mit Verständnisproblemen

Die Lesetexte in der Abschlussprüfung enthalten manchmal Wörter, die du nicht kennst, und ein Wörterbuch ist nicht erlaubt. Aber keine Angst! Mit den richtigen Strategien kannst du die Aufgaben oft trotzdem richtig lösen. Wenn du auf ein unbekanntes Wort triffst, kannst du es zunächst markieren und versuchen, es dir zu erschließen, z. B. aus dem Zusammenhang oder durch ähnliche Wörter, die du kennst. Bei einigen Aufgaben genügt es auch, wenn du die allgemeine Aussage des Textes verstehst, selbst wenn du nicht jedes Wort kennst. Dieses Kapitel präsentiert einige wichtige Strategien anhand eines Sachtextes über die Everglades.

The Everglades

The Everglades are a region of tropical wetlands in southern Florida. This text is taken from a local government brochure that gives the reasons why there will be road works on an important road in the Everglades.

> Neu – kannst du den Sinn aus bekannten Wörtern erschließen? Vielleicht ist es aber für deine Antwort auch unwichtig!

> Vielleicht neu – aber du kannst die Bedeutung aus dem Zusammenhang erschließen: Es geht um den Lebensraum der Alligatoren.

1   The wetlands of the Everglades in the south of the state of Florida are famous for their alligators, snakes, turtles and other wildlife, which tourists can sometimes catch sight of from airboats or on
5   specially-provided hiking trails. Visitor centers show alligators feeding and inform tourists about how the alligators' environment is endangered.

> Neu – aber aus dem Zusammenhang kannst du schließen: Die Haustiere sind in den Everglades, weil die Menschen sie herausgelassen haben.

> Neu – aber du kennst *danger* = Gefahr.

2   In fact, the Everglades are facing huge environmental issues. Its lakes and rivers are polluted by
10   dirty waste water from the city of Miami. And pets released into the Everglades by inhabitants of the city have become a danger to the original wildlife.

> Du kennst *wet* und *land*. Was könnten also *wetlands* sein?

3   But the biggest headache of all is that the wetlands are drying out. This is partly because, in the
15   1960s, the slow-flowing Kissimmee River was replaced by a dead straight canal that makes the water flow away too quickly. And what makes it worse is that the U.S. Highway 41, which was completed in 1928, cuts through 275 miles of the Everglades from
20   east to west on a wall of earth. This prevents water from flowing into the southern part of the Everglades.

> Neues Verb – aber du kennst *dry* = trocken.

> Neu – aber aus dem Zusammenhang kannst du schließen: Dieser Erdwall hindert das Wasser am Fließen.

4   It has now been decided that parts of the canal will be filled in to allow the water to flow into the slower river. And a mile-long stretch of Highway 41 will be
25   made into a bridge to allow water to pass under it.

1. Read the brochure about the Everglades on page 31. **Match the headings (A–E) with the paragraphs (1–4)** and write the correct numbers in the boxes. Use each number only once. Be careful, there is **one heading** that you do **not need**.

A The beauty of the Everglades ☐

B Pollution problems ☐

C Educating the public ☐

D What is being done to help ☐

E Past mistakes ☐

Tipp

Wie kannst du eine Überschrift zuordnen, wenn du nicht alle Wörter kennst?
Beispiel: In Überschrift **B** kennst du *pollution* vielleicht nicht. Keine Panik:
1. In zwei Absätzen geht es um Probleme, nämlich _____ und _____. So grenzt du die Auswahl ein.
2. Zu einem dieser beiden Absätze passt auch eine andere Überschrift. Es geht darin um die Vergangenheit. Das ist Absatz _____.

Also gehört Überschrift **B** wahrscheinlich zu Absatz _____.

2. Read the text again. Are sentences 1–5 *True* (T) or *False* (F)? Choose *Not in the text* (N) if there is not enough information to answer *True* or *False*. **Tick (✓) the correct answer.**

		T	F	N
1	Luckily the environment in which the alligators live is not really in danger.	☐	☐	☐
2	People from Miami sometimes try to catch wild animals in the Everglades.	☐	☐	☐
3	The wetlands of the Everglades aren't getting enough water.	☐	☐	☐
4	A highway was built through the Everglades in the 19th century.	☐	☐	☐
5	The plan now is to build a bridge over the Highway, so that the water can flow better.	☐	☐	☐

Tipp

Sätze 1+3: Was ist, wenn du die entscheidenden Textstellen nicht verstanden hast, weil du einige Wörter nicht kennst? Denke an Wortfamilien:

Familie *danger*: *danger* (Nomen), *dangerous* (Adjektiv), *to endanger* (Verb), ...

Familie *wet*: *wet* (Adjektiv), *to wet* (Verb), *wetness* (Nomen), *wet-look* (Nomen), *wetlands* (Nomen), ...

Familie *dry*: *dry* (Adjektiv), *hairdryer* (Nomen), *to dry (out)* (Verb), ...

So kannst du dir den Sinn der entscheidenden Sätze erschließen und die Aufgabe lösen. Natürlich hilft dir hier auch der Zusammenhang weiter.

Tipp

Satz 2: Die entscheidende Stelle ist Absatz **2**, aber du kennst *release* nicht? Versuche, dir den Sinn des Satzes auch ohne *release* zu erschließen:

... pets ... have become a danger to the original wildlife.

Die Haustiere der Bewohner von Miami bringen also Wildtiere in Gefahr. Es ist aber keine Rede davon, dass die Bewohner von Miami Wildtiere fangen. Also ist der Satz _____.

Tipp

Satz 4: Du hast gelernt, dass Zahlen auf verschiedene Weisen ausgedrückt werden können. Entspricht die Jahreszahl aus dem Text *(in 1928)* der Angabe in der Aufgabe *(in the 19th century)*? Hier hilft dir dein Weltwissen: 1928 war im ...

☐ 18. Jh. ☐ 19. Jh. ☐ 20 Jh.

3. Verwende die Informationen aus der Broschüre über die Everglades. **Bearbeite die Aufgaben (1–3) stichpunktartig auf Deutsch**. Es ist keine wörtliche Übersetzung nötig, die Aspekte müssen **inhaltlich** jedoch **vollständig** erfasst sein. Einzelwörter genügen nicht als Antwort.

1 Was können die Touristen in den Besucherzentren erleben und lernen? **(2 Aspekte)**

_____

_____

2 Wie tragen die Einwohner von Miami zu den Problemen bei? **(2 Aspekte)**

_____

_____

3 Was plant die Regierung, um die Umweltprobleme zu beheben? **(2 Aspekte)**

_____

_____

Written Test, Part II: Use of English (Wortschatz, Grammatik)

Die schriftliche Prüfung *(Written Test)* besteht aus drei Teilen:
* Part I: Leseverstehen *(Reading)*
* **Part II: Wortschatz und Grammatik** *(Use of English)*
* Part III: gelenktes Schreiben *(Guided Writing)*

Für diese drei schriftlichen Prüfungsteile hast du insgesamt 105 Minuten Zeit. Du kannst dir diese Zeit selbst einteilen. Plane also genügend Zeit für jeden Teil ein und bedenke dabei, dass du am Ende auch noch Zeit zum Korrekturlesen benötigst.

1. Ablauf und Bewertung

Im zweiten Teil der schriftlichen Prüfung werden deine Fertigkeiten in den Bereichen Wortschatz und Grammatik geprüft. Alle Aufgaben werden im Kontext angeboten, nehmen also entweder auf einen Lesetext Bezug oder erscheinen in ganzen Sätzen.

Folgende Aufgabenformate sind üblich:
* Synonyme finden
* Wörtern die richtige Bedeutung zuordnen
* die richtige Form eines vorgegebenen Wortes bilden
* anhand von vorgegebenen *key words* Sätze umformulieren
* Lücken in einem Text mit Wörtern in der korrekten Form füllen

Bei *Use of English* kannst du maximal 30 Punkte erreichen. Das sind 20% der gesamten Prüfungsnote. Deine Antworten werden entweder als richtig oder falsch bewertet, halbe Punkte sind nicht möglich.

Auch bei *Use of English* ist ein Wörterbuch <u>nicht</u> erlaubt. Alle Rechtschreib- und Grammatikfehler, die du in diesem Prüfungsteil machst, führen zu einem Punktverlust.

2. Typische Aufgabenformate

In diesem Kapitel lernst du die Textsorten und Aufgabenformate kennen, die dich bei der Realschulabschlussprüfung in Bayern im Bereich *Use of English* am häufigsten erwarten.

Beachte: Die ersten beiden Aufgaben im Bereich *Use of English* beziehen sich in der Prüfung meist auf den langen Lesetext aus dem Prüfungsteil *Reading*. Hier in der *Training Section* werden die Aufgabenformate beispielhaft anhand von eigenen, meist kürzeren Texten vorgestellt. Wortschatz- und Grammatikaufgaben auf der Grundlage des langen *Reading*-Textes findest du in den Musterprüfungen.

Die Tipp-Kästen enthalten nützliche Hinweise und Hilfen.

Indian food in Britain

Indian cooking has been popular in Britain for longer than many people realize: a British cookery book in 1774 contained numerous recipes for Indian dishes. Many British people were familiar with Indian food because Britain governed India, and a huge number of British people lived there.

In the early 20th century, more and more Indian seamen reached Britain's shores. Many decided to stay and run small restaurants. The men were often from areas in Bangladesh and Pakistan. This was all part of British India back then, so the food was called Indian food. The cafe owners soon noticed that people returning from late shifts at work wanted to buy hot food before getting the bus home. They did not have time to sit down and eat; they wanted their meals in a form that they could carry. This was the birth of the *Indian take-away*.

While for years *chicken tikka masala* was the best-selling dish served in Indian take-aways, customers are now trying out a wider range of dishes. One reason for this is the enormous influence of TV food programmes and food blogs: customers are now more informed about the range of food available. It also reflects people's concerns about their own health, with many customers looking for lower-calorie dishes.

Find a synonym – a word or expression which means the same

Bei der ersten Aufgabe im Bereich *Use of English* geht es um Wortschatz. Deine Aufgabe besteht darin, aus einem Lesetext Wörter oder Wendungen herauszusuchen, die dasselbe bedeuten wie die (meist fünf) vorgegebenen Wörter. Die Zeilenangaben weisen dich auf den Textabschnitt hin, in dem du das gesuchte Wort oder die gesuchte Wendung finden kannst.

> Look at the text *Indian food in Britain*. **Find a word or expression which means <u>the same as</u> each of the words (1–5) below.** The lines where you can find the words or expressions are indicated in brackets. There is one example **(0)** at the beginning.

0 well-liked → *popular* (l. 1–7)

1 very large → _____ (l. 1–7)

2 (to) rule → _____ (l. 1–7)

> **Tipp**
>
> **Wort 2:** Bei Verben wird in der Prüfung meist der Infinitiv angegeben. Bei deiner Antwort wird der Infinitiv des gesuchten Verbs akzeptiert, aber auch die Verbform, die im Text erscheint, hier also entweder *(to)* _ _ _ _ _ _ _ oder
> _ _ _ _ _ _ _ _ _ .

> **Tipp**
>
> Bei diesem Aufgabenformat hilft Folgendes:
> 1. Überlege, um welche Wortart (Nomen, Verb, Adjektiv, Adverb ...) es sich handelt. Suche dann nach derselben Wortart im Text.
> 2. Prüfe, ob das gefundene Wort dieselbe Bedeutung hat.
>
>   Beispiel: Die Wörter **0** und **1** sind Adjektive. Also musst du im Text nach Adjektiven suchen. Notiere die fünf Adjektive in diesem Absatz: *popular, longer, ...*
>
> → *longer* fällt aus, weil es eine Steigerungsform ist.
> → Es bleiben also vier Möglichkeiten, und damit ist deine Aufgabe schon leichter.
>
> 3. Setze zum Schluss das ursprünglich vorgegebene Wort an der gefundenen Stelle ein. Passt es?

3 (a) region → _____ (l. 8–19)

4 (an) effect → _____ (l. 20–29)

5 (a) worry → _____ (l. 20–29)

Match expressions with definitions

Bei der zweiten Aufgabe im Bereich Wortschatz geht es darum, Begriffen aus dem Lesetext die passende Bedeutung zuzuordnen. In den vergangenen Jahren kamen dabei zwei Aufgabenformate zum Einsatz, die beide hier vorgestellt werden. Im folgenden Beispiel sollst du vorgegebenen Wörtern die richtige aus einer (meist größeren) Auswahl an Definitionen zuordnen *(Matching)*.

Look at the text *Indian food in Britain* again. What do the following words mean? **Match** the expressions (B–F) with their corresponding definitions (1–8). **Write the correct numbers in the grid below.** Be careful: There are two definitions that you do not need. One definition has already been matched correctly.

A	**to contain** (l. 3)	
B	to govern (l. 6)	
C	to reach (l. 9)	
D	to notice (l. 14)	
E	to return (l. 14)	
F	to carry (l. 18)	

1 to go back

2 to make a comment about something

3 **to have in it**

4 to take something in your hand and take it to another place

5 to see

6 to arrive in a place after a long or hard journey

7 to make something known to somebody

8 to rule and make the laws

A	B	C	D	E	F
3					

Underline the best German translation

Auch das folgende Aufgabenformat kann dir bei der zweiten Aufgabe im Bereich Wortschatz begegnen. Wieder geht es darum, Wörtern aus dem Lesetext die richtige Bedeutung zuzuordnen. Doch statt der Definitionen erhältst du diesmal Wörterbuch-Einträge. Du sollst die Übersetzungsmöglichkeit unterstreichen, die am besten in den Textzusammenhang passt.

> The following words have various meanings. Which of the meanings given in the dictionary is the one used in the text *Indian food in Britain*? **Underline** the best German translation.

run *(l. 10)*
n **1.** Lauf *She went for a run.*
v. intr **1.** laufen, rennen
2. (Wasser etc.) laufen, fließen **3.** kandidieren
He's running for president.
v. trans **1.** einlaufen lassen
(a bath) **2.** etw. leiten, führen, betreiben **3.** erledigen
(errands)

get *(l. 16)*
v. intr **1.** werden *It's getting dark.* **2.** kommen, ankommen
We got to London at about 9.
3. geraten *(into trouble)*
v. trans **1.** etw. bekommen
2. etw. holen, abholen
3. nehmen *(bus, train)*
4. verstehen, mitbekommen
Sorry, I didn't get that.

range *(l. 26)*
v. intr schwanken, sich bewegen *(temperature, price, age)*
n **1.** Reihe, Sortiment *They offer a wide range of products.*
2. Spannbreite, Vielfalt, Auswahl **3.** *no pl (AmE)*
Weidefläche **4.** Schussweite
5. *(mountains)* Kette

Tipp

Alle im Wörterbuch genannten Übersetzungen sind grundsätzlich für das Wort richtig. Aber nicht alle passen in den Zusammenhang des Textes. Bei manchen Bedeutungen passt nicht einmal die Wortart. Lies also unbedingt noch einmal die entsprechende Textstelle. Vielleicht hilft es dir, die Textstelle im Kopf zu übersetzen und dabei die Bedeutungen aus dem Wörterbuch einzusetzen. Dann merkst du, welche am besten passt.

Form a word of the same word family

Bei der dritten Aufgabe im Prüfungsteil *Use of English* geht es um Wortschatz und Grammatik. Du erhältst einen Lückentext mit vorgegebenen Wörtern in Großbuchstaben am Rand. Deine Aufgabe besteht darin, ein Wort derselben Wortfamilie in der grammatikalisch richtigen Form in die jeweilige Lücke einzusetzen, sodass der Text einen Sinn ergibt.

Tipp

Wortfamilien
Wörter verschiedener Wortarten können „Familien" bilden. Sie haben dann denselben Stamm, aber je nach Wortart unterschiedliche Vorsilben oder Endungen. Beispiel:
*to **help**, **help**er, **help**ful, **help**less* gehören zu einer Wortfamilie und haben den gemeinsamen Wortstamm *help*.

> Use the word given in capitals at the end of some of the lines to **form a word of the same word family** that fits in the space in the same line. There is one example **(0)** at the beginning.

Tipp

1. Stelle zuerst fest, welche Wortart in der Lücke benötigt wird: ein Verb, ein Nomen, ein Adjektiv, ein Adverb?

2. Verwandle entsprechend das vorgegebene Wort am Rand. Beachte dabei, dass Nomen in der Einzahl oder Mehrzahl stehen können, dass Verben eine Vielzahl an Formen bilden können (*-s*, *-ed*, *-ing*, unregelmäßige Formen, ...), dass bei Adjektiven eine Steigerungsform verlangt sein kann etc.

Zum Beispiel:
In **0** brauchst du einen **Nomen**. Das Nomen zu *busy* ist *business*.
In **1** brauchst du ein **Verb**. In einem Satz mit *for 100 years* brauchst du das *Present perfect = have* _ _ _ _ _ _.

K&J Logistics (formerly Liptons Removals)

0 We are a local *business*.   BUSY

1 We have _____ people to move house for 100 years.   HELPFUL

2 We are a trusted and _____ company and are   RELIABILITY

3 happy to give you _____ advice. If you are   USE

4 thinking of _____ house, we will do everything   MOVE

5 possible to make this an _____ experience for you.   ENJOY

6 In the last few years we have _____ a new line in   DEVELOPMENT

7 renting out vans. Please find us online.

Tipp

Prüfe bei jedem Wort, welche Wortart der Text verlangt. Bilde dann aus dem vorgegebenen Wort die richtige Form aus derselben Wortfamilie:

	vorgegebenes Wort	verlangte Wortart	richtige Form (= deine Lösung)
0	busy	*Nomen*	*business*
1	helpful	*Verb (present perfect)*	*(have)* _ _ _ _ _ _
2	reliability	*Adjektiv*	
3	use		
4	move		
5	enjoy		
6	development		

Complete the sentences using the key word

Bei der vierten Aufgabe im Prüfungsteil *Use of English* geht es ebenfalls um Wortschatz und Grammatik. Du sollst vorgegebene Sätze so umformulieren, dass ihr Sinn erhalten bleibt. Für die neue Formulierung erhältst du einen Satzanfang und einen Schlüsselbegriff *(key word)*, den du verwenden musst, aber nicht verändern darfst. In der Prüfung sind meist vier bis fünf Sätze umzuwandeln. Hier sind es zu Trainingszwecken mehr Aufgaben, die die häufigsten Strukturen abdecken.

Complete the second sentence so that it has a similar meaning to the first sentence, using the KEY WORD given in brackets. **Do not change the KEY WORD given. You must use between two and five words including the KEY WORD.** There is one example **(0)** at the beginning.

Top sights in London: The Shard

0 London's tallest skyscraper was built by the Italian architect Renzo Piano. **(WHO)**

It was the Italian architect Renzo Piano *who built* London's tallest skyscraper.

Tipp

In Satz **0** geht es um die Umwandlung eines vorgegebenen Passivsatzes in einen Aktivsatz mithilfe des vorgegebenen Relativpronomens WHO.

Es könnte in der Prüfung aber auch genau das Umgekehrte von dir verlangt werden. Es ist ein Aktivsatz vorgegeben und du sollst ihn mithilfe von BY in einen Passivsatz umwandeln:

The Italian architect Renzo Piano built London's tallest skyscraper. (BY)

London's tallest skyscraper _____ *the Italian architect Renzo Piano.*

→ Bei diesem Aufgabentyp ist …
  … WHO oft ein Signalwort für die Umwandlung vom Passiv ins Aktiv.
  … BY oft ein Signalwort für die Umwandlung vom Aktiv ins Passiv.

→ Empfohlene Wiederholung: Passivsätze!

---

1 People say that the building looks like a giant piece of glass: a shard. **(SAID)**

The building _____
like a giant piece of glass: a shard.

Tipp

Achtung! Das Keyword SAID deutet in **Satz 1** nicht auf die Vergangenheit, sondern es ist Teil einer Passivkonstruktion!
Auch hier geht es also um Aktiv/Passiv: Aus dem aktivischen *People say …* soll mithilfe von SAID ein eher unpersönlicher Passivsatz werden.

2 Lay all the glass together and you cover six football fields. **(IF)**

_____ all the glass
together, you would cover six football fields.

Tipp

Bei den **Sätzen 2–4** musst du *if*-Sätze bilden.

→ Empfohlene Wiederholung: *if*-Sätze!

3 No building in Germany is taller than The Shard. **(IT)**

If The Shard was in Germany, _____

_____ the tallest building in the country.

4 I really think that you should visit The Shard. **(WERE)**

_____ I would
visit The Shard.

Tipp

Weitere häufige grammatische Themen bei diesem Aufgabenformat sind die *tenses* und das *gerund*.

Bei **Satz 5** geht es um die korrekte Verwendung der *tenses*:

FOR *(10 years / 5 days / many weeks / …)* ist ein Signal für das _____.

Bei **Satz 6** sollst du ein *gerund (Not wanting to …)* in einen Nebensatz mit BECAUSE umwandeln. Da der Hauptsatz *(chose)* im _ _ _ _ _ _ _ _ _ _ _ steht, muss auch dein Nebensatz in dieser Zeit stehen.

5 It's at least sixty years since high-rise buildings began to be built in London. **(FOR)**

In London, high-rise buildings _____

_____ at least sixty years.

6 Not wanting to seem old-fashioned, Renzo Piano chose a new shape for his skyscraper. **(BECAUSE)**

Renzo Piano chose a new shape for his

skyscraper _____ _____

_____ to seem old-fashioned.

7 People in London often see tall
buildings. **(USED)**

People in London _____

_____ tall buildings.

But The Shard stands out among them.

8 It's so tall that seeing places 40 miles away is
possible from its top. **(ABLE)**

It's so tall that some people _____

_____ places 40 miles away from its top.

9 In fact, the architect's hope was that people
would notice The Shard from a long distance.
(WANTED)

In fact, the architect _____

_____ The Shard from a long distance.

Renzo Piano's hopes were fulfilled, but some

Londoners aren't happy about this because

now The Shard blocks the view of other

popular London sights.

Tipp

Bei **Satz 7** zwingt dich das Keyword USED, selbst ein
gerund zu benutzen.

→ Empfohlene Wiederholung:
die *tenses* und das *gerund*!

Tipp

Manche Verben ziehen einen einfachen Infinitiv
nach sich, andere *to* + Infinitiv oder ein *gerund* (-ing).
Auch dies ist häufig Thema dieses Aufgabenformats.

In **Satz 8** wird wieder eine vorgegebene *gerund*-
Konstruktion *(... seeing places ...)* aufgelöst, nämlich
durch das Keyword ABLE:
It's so tall that some people are able ...

Der gleiche Satz könnte auch durch andere
Keywords umgewandelt werden. Vergleiche:
(CAN): *... some people can ...*
(SUCCEED): *... some people succeed ...*

Woher weißt du nun, was hinter dem vorgegebenen Verb/Keyword kommt? Da es dafür kaum
Regeln gibt, solltest du bei häufigen Verben gleich
ihre üblichen Verbindungen mitlernen. Du kannst
auch Listen anlegen:

Verb + Infinitiv: *can do, must do, let (sb.) do, ...*

Verb + *to* + Infinitiv: *be able to do, be allowed to do,
manage to do, want (sb.) to do, hope to do, ...*

Verb (+ Präposition) + *gerund*: *succeed in doing,
used to doing, enjoy doing, be fed up with doing, ...*

Bei manchen Verben gibt es auch mehrere
Möglichkeiten:
They like to do ... / They like doing ...
They hate to do ... / They hate doing ...
They start to do ... / They start doing ...

London Skyline with Tower Bridge and Shard Skyscraper

Complete the text (gapped text)

Bei der fünften Aufgabe im Bereich *Use of English* geht es überwiegend um Grammatik. Du erhältst einen Text mit Lücken, die du füllen musst. Hinter einigen Lücken ist ein Wort vorgegeben, das du in die grammatikalisch richtige Form bringen musst. Hinter anderen Lücken gibt es Fragezeichen: Hier sollst du selbst das (inhaltlich und grammatikalisch) passende Wort finden. Vorsicht: Es kann mehr als nur ein Wort verlangt werden.

> **Complete the following text.** Use the correct forms of the words in brackets and find words of your own to replace the question marks. There is one example **(0)** at the beginning.

Most parents give their **(0)** *children* **(child)** pocket

money. Mine give me money, but it's never

enough **(1)** _____ **(???)** what I need.

So you would have thought **(2)** _____

(???) my parents would be happy that I have found

a job in a clothes shop. But they **(3)** _____

(not / be). They constantly complain about my job.

They say that if I have a job I'll be too tired for

school and for **(4)** _____ **(do)** my

homework, even though no teacher has ever

complained **(5)** _____ **(???)** my school

work. They say that the music in the shop is

louder **(6)** _____ **(???)** it should be.

They say that our shop **(7)** _____ **(???)**

cheap clothes that **(8)** _____

(make) in Bangladesh, where men, women and children often work in terrible conditions for very

(9) _____ **(???)** pay. They would prefer it, they say, if I **(10)** _____ **(work)** in

a Fairtrade shop that sends money back to the workers **(11)** _____ **(???)** make the products.

Tipp

Bei Verben (Lücken **3**, **4**, **7**, **8**, **10**) überlege immer:
- Welche Zeitform *(tense)*?
- Aktiv oder Passiv?
- Einzahl oder Mehrzahl?
- Bejaht oder verneint?
- Regelmäßig oder unregelmäßig?
- -s im *simple present* bei *he/she/it*

Tipp

0 Vorsicht: unregelmäßige Pluralform!

1 Welche Präposition wird hier verlangt?

2 Welches Wort verbindet die beiden Satzteile?

5 Welche Präposition nach *complain*?

6 Bei einem Vergleich (Komparativ) brauchst du welches Wort?

7 Hier musst du ein Verb vorschlagen. Was macht der Laden mit den Kleidungsstücken?

9 Das englische Wort für „wenig"?

11 Welches Wort verbindet die zwei Satzteile?

Weitere häufige Strukturen bei diesem Aufgabenformat: Genitive, *if*-Sätze, indirekte Rede, Adjektiv/Adverb, …

Prüfungsvorbereitung

- **Beginne rechtzeitig mit dem Lernen und mache dir einen Lernplan**, bei dem du auch Wiederholungsphasen einplanst. Starte mit Aufgaben, die dir im Unterricht noch schwer fallen. Hake ab, was du bereits erledigt hast.

- **Überlege dir, wo du im Englischen noch grundsätzliche Probleme oder Lücken hast** (z.B. Grammatikprobleme, die immer wieder auftreten). Diese Themen kannst du dann mit den interaktiven Übungen auf www.scook.de gezielt noch einmal wiederholen.

- **Mache dich mit dem Ablauf der Prüfung und mit allen Aufgabenformaten vertraut**. Plane im Vorfeld, wie viel Zeit du für jeden Prüfungsteil und für die Kontrolle zur Verfügung hast.

- **Schreibe dir auf, wann und wo die Prüfung stattfindet**, und plane etwas mehr Zeit für den Weg ein als sonst.

- **Lege alle Materialien am Vorabend der Prüfung bereit** (z.B. funktionstüchtige Stifte, Uhr; Smartphones sind nicht erlaubt!).

- **Achte auf ausreichend Schlaf und ein gutes Frühstück.**

Wenn du dich gut vorbereitet hast, kannst du selbstbewusst in die Prüfung gehen!

Während der Prüfung

- **Behalte die Zeit im Blick!** Am besten legst du während der Prüfung eine Uhr auf den Tisch und schaust von Zeit zu Zeit darauf. Wenn du an einer Aufgabe festhängst, gehe lieber erstmal zur nächsten Frage weiter. Nimm dir am Ende einige Minuten Zeit, um deine Antworten noch einmal durchzugehen.

- **Lies die Aufgabenstellung gründlich durch**, bevor du mit der Bearbeitung beginnst. Manchmal enthält eine Aufgabe mehrere Teilaspekte. Markiere sie und übersetze sie dir zur Sicherheit in deine Muttersprache.

- **Nutze deine Chance!** Auch wenn du unsicher bist, ob die Lösung stimmt, so ist es ratsam, die Aufgabe trotzdem zu bearbeiten. So hast du zumindest eine Chance, dass es richtig ist. Kreuzt du keine Lösung an oder lässt die Lücke leer, so bekommst du auf jeden Fall null Punkte. Kreuzt du aber mehr Lösungen an als gefordert, so verlierst du ebenfalls Punkte.

- **Mache dir bei Schreibaufgaben Notizen, wenn du gut in der Zeit liegst.** Sie können dir helfen, deine Gedanken zu ordnen und deinen Text sinnvoll zu strukturieren. Beachte aber, dass nur dein endgültiger Text in die Bewertung eingeht.

- **Gib deinen Texten eine gute Struktur mit Einleitung, Hauptteil und Schluss.** Beginne jeden neuen Textteil mit einem neuen Absatz. Halte dich ungefähr an die geforderte Textlänge.

- **Formuliere klare Sätze.** Vermeide es, komplizierte deutsche Sätze wortwörtlich ins Englische zu übersetzen. Formuliere möglichst mit deinen eigenen Worten.

- **Kontrolliere am Ende**, was du geschrieben hast. Achte besonders auf Vollständigkeit, die Rechtschreibung, die Zeitformen deiner Verben und den Satzbau.

Wir wünschen dir viel Erfolg für deine Prüfung!

▶ **Fortsetzung der *Training Section* (Seite 43) nach den Lösungen**

ABSCHLUSS-
PRÜFUNGS-
TRAINER

Realschulabschluss
Bayern

Lösungen

TRAINING SECTION: Listening Test ▶ p. 14

Matching: Radio ads
A 3 · B / · C 2 · D / · E 4 · F 1

Multiple choice: A visit to Krakow
1 B (**Tipp:** airport, fly, flight …)

2 C (**Tipp:** A und B)

3 A (**Tipp:** Die Formulierung im Hörtext ist negativ: not the main tourist sites)

4 B (**Tipp:** use your hands = making signs)

5 B

Error spotting: A tourist attraction in Brighton
flowers → towers · 1850 → 1815 · walking → working · thinking → drinking · should → could · viewed → food

Note taking: Bob Marley
1 February 1945
2 18 years old / She was 18.
3 60 years old / He was 60.
4 The Teenagers
5 No Woman, No Cry / Buffalo Soldier / I Shot the Sheriff / Concrete Jungle / Simmer Down
6 he took drugs/cannabis; he fought for independence of African countries / got involved in politics

Note taking / Sentence completion: A guided tour of Bo-Kaap
1 There were Muslims in South Africa in 1794 because Europeans brought workers from south-east Asia. / they were brought from India. / they were brought to work there. / they were forced to come and work in Cape Town. / …

2 The number of Asian South Africans today is over one million. / more than a million. / …

3 Outside of Cape Town, Asian workers worked in sugar fields or coal mines.

4 At the Bo-Kaap museum you can see the old furniture of Asian families. / the furniture of Muslim families in the 19th century. / …

5 Bo-Kaap has changed in the last few years. For example,
  – other people have started to move there. / …
  – it has become more multicultural. / people are beginning to mix. / …
  – neighbours don't know their neighbours anymore. / …
  – people don't share the same culture anymore. / …
  (zwei von mehreren möglichen inhaltlichen Aspekten)

Multiple choice: The Niagara Falls (Part 1)
1 C (**Tipp:** Buffalo ist eine Stadt und liegt 30 Autominuten von den Niagarafällen entfernt.; D scheidet auch aus, da nur die beiden kleineren Wasserfälle komplett in den USA liegen.; But these amazing falls, called the Horseshoe Falls, are the biggest and they're mainly in Canada.) · 2 C

Error spotting: The Niagara Falls (Part 2)
light → sight · share → care · county's → country's · made → laid · land → stand

Note taking / Sentence completion: The Niagara Falls (Part 3)
1 Annie Taylor went over the falls in order to raise money. / earn money. / sell her story. / … (**Tipp:** Sie war arm. / Sie brauchte Geld.)

2 She asked the first group of friends to put her in the water. / push her towards the falls. / push the barrel into the water / into the falls / in the right direction at the top. / …

3 After her experiment, Annie warned other people against doing the same thing. / people not to do this. / that it was too dangerous. / …

TRAINING SECTION: Part I: Reading ▶ p. 22

Australia's Stolen Generations
True, false or not in the text?
Tipps:

	im Text:	in der Aufgabe:	Bedeutung gleich oder ähnlich?
1	rule	law	ja
	… take (…) children away from their mothers and fathers	… children to be removed from their families	ja
	in 1915	in the early 20th century	ja
2	250,000 to 500,000	more than half a million	nein
	from their mothers and fathers	from their parents	ja
4	families, language, music, way of life	culture	ja
	had no contact with	lost touch	ja

1 true · 2 false · 3 not in the text · 4 true

Matching (headings and paragraphs)
A 3 · B 1 · C / · D 2 · E 4

Kasun
Matching (removed sentences and gaps)
A 3 · B 1 · C 5 · D 4

My favourite British planes

Sequencing (Put into the correct order)

Tipp: Der erste Teil des Textes mit dem *topic sentence* ist Textteil **B**.

1	2	3	4	5	6	7
B	F	A	D	G	C	E

Matching (statements/questions and objects)

1 C · 2 B · 3 C · 4 A · 5 A · 6 B

The Isle of Man TT Race

Error spotting (Write the words which should not be there on the lines...)

1 had · 2 / · 3 of · 4 that · 5 the · 6 / · 7 absolute · 8 / · 9 wanted · 10 /

Filming in New Zealand

Mediation

Hinweis: Andere Formulierungen sind zulässig, solange der inhaltliche Aspekt (im Lösungsbeispiel unterstrichen) korrekt erfasst ist.

1 Die spektakuläre (beeindruckende/atemberaubende/...) Landschaft (Natur) und die fortschrittliche Technologie (die guten Special-Effects-Firmen / die Qualität der technischen Nachbearbeitung / ...) ziehen internationale Filmemacher nach Neuseeland.

2 Der Film wurde in spektakulären (wilden/abgelegenen/bergigen/...) Nationalparks und in den sanften (weniger dramatischen / ...) Hügeln (nahe Matamata) gefilmt.

3 Neuseeland ist ungefähr so groß wie Großbritannien.

4 Auch Hubschrauberpiloten (eine Hubschrauberfirma) und Tricktechniker (Computerspezialisten / Grafikdesigner / Spezialeffekte-Techniker / ...) profitierten von dem Film.

5 Die Firma filmte einen Drachen im Flug (flog einen Hubschrauber, aus dem ein Drache gefilmt wurde. / ...).

6 Wellington war Drehort für *King Kong* (stellt in *King Kong* New York dar. / ...).

The Everglades

1: A / · B 2 · C 1 · D 4 · E 3 (**Tipp:** 1. Absätze 2 und 3; 2. Absatz 3; Absatz 2)

2: 1 false · 2 not in the text · 3 true · 4 false · 5 false (**Tipp:** 20 Jh.)

3: **Hinweis:** Andere Formulierungen sind zulässig, solange der inhaltliche Aspekt (im Lösungsbeispiel unterstrichen) korrekt erfasst ist.

1 Sie erleben (sehen/...), wie Alligatoren gefüttert werden (was Alligatoren essen / ...), und erfahren (lernen/...), wie die Umwelt der Alligatoren gefährdet ist.

2 Ihr schmutziges (dreckiges/...) (Ab-)wasser verdreckt (verpestet/...) das Wasser (die Seen und Flüsse) in den Everglades, und ihre Haustiere gefährden die Tiere der Everglades.

3 Die Regierung plant (hat vor), den Kanal teilweise wieder aufzufüllen und einen Teil des Highway 41 auf eine Brücke zu setzen.

TRAINING SECTION: Part II: Use of English ▶ p. 34

Indian food in Britain

Find a synonym – a word or expression which means the same

1 huge (**Tipp:** popular, longer, numerous, familiar, huge) · 2 (to) govern / governed · 3 area/areas (**Tipp:** Nomen) · 4 influence · 5 concern/concerns

Match expressions with definitions

A	B	C	D	E	F
3	8	6	5	1	4

Underline the best German translation

run: hier: leiten, führen, betreiben · get: hier: nehmen · range: hier: Spannbreite, Vielfalt, Auswahl

Form a word of the same word family

Tipp/Lösung:

	vorgegebenes Wort	verlangte Wortart	richtige Form (= deine Lösung)
0	busy	Nomen	business
1	helpful	Verb (present perfect)	(have) helped
2	reliability	Adjektiv	reliable
3	use	Adjektiv	useful/us(e)able
4	move	Verb (gerund)	moving
5	enjoy	Adjektiv	enjoyable
6	development	Verb (present perfect)	(have) developed

Complete the sentences using the key word

Tipp: London's tallest skyscraper was built by the Italian architect Renzo Piano.

1 The building is said to look like a giant piece of glass: a shard.

2 If you laid all the glass together, you would cover six football fields.

3 If The Shard was in Germany, it would be the tallest building in the country.

4 If I were you, I would visit The Shard.

5 In London, high-rise buildings have been built for at least sixty years. (**Tipp:** FOR 10 years / 5 days / ... ist ein Signal für das present perfect.)

6 Renzo Piano chose a new shape for his skyscraper because he didn't want (it) to seem old-fashioned. (**Tipp:** Der Hauptsatz steht im simple past.)

7 People in London are used to seeing tall buildings.

8 It's so tall that some people are able to see places 40 miles away from its top. (**Tipp:** are able to see / can see / succeed in seeing)

9 In fact, the architect wanted people to notice The Shard from a long distance.

Complete the text (gapped text)

1 for · **2** that · **3** aren't / are not · **4** doing · **5** about · **6** than · **7** sells/offers · **8** have been made / were made / are made · **9** little/poor/low · **10** worked · **11** who/that

---

TRAINING SECTION: Part III: Guided Writing ▶ p. 43

Personal emails

Schritt 1:

Persönliche E-Mails	
Anrede	Dear (+name), Hi (+ name), Hi there!, Hello, Hey, …
Schluss	Bye for now, Love, Best wishes, Kind regards, …

Schritt 2:

Dear Danny

Thanks for your mail – that's awesome news! I've been thinking a lot about your question.

Munich or a Bavarian farm – if you ask me, I'd choose Munich! (aspect **3** mentioned) Think of all the exciting shops, the cinemas, the cafes. (included) A farm, however, is not so much different from a farm in England … (elaborated)

What's more, your aim was to improve your German. (aspect **1** mentioned) In Munich you would meet tons of people (included), whereas on a farm you might often be on your own and so it could be more difficult for you to practise your German. (elaborated) As a result, your German wouldn't improve very much. (fully elaborated)

On the other hand, farm work would probably be more your kind of thing because you're an outside person. (aspect **2** mentioned) And you're really good with animals! (included) But then again, the animals won't talk to you (elaborated) and farm work can be exhausting, especially in awful weather! (fully elaborated)

And finally, don't forget about your free time. (aspect **4** mentioned) If you were in Munich you could explore the city and chat with people. (included) Besides, if you had a couple of days free, you could easily get on a train and visit me! (elaborated) Or else you could spend the weekend in the mountains and do the outside activities that you love. (fully elaborated)

So all in all I would recommend the job in town. Does this help you? Good luck, and I hope we'll be able to meet when you come to Germany!

Love,
Nurit (239 words)

Inhalt: Alle vier Aspekte sind angesprochen und drei davon voll ausgearbeitet: 7 Punkte

Aufbau und Zusammenhang:

Verbindungswörter und -phrasen	
Funktion	Beispiel
Informationen/Gedanken/… hinzufügen	what's more, and, besides
Die Reihenfolge verdeutlichen	finally
Gegenteil/Kontrast ausdrücken	however, on the other hand, whereas, but then again, or else
Begründung/Zweck anführen	because
Gedankengänge abschließen	as a result, so, and so
Ein Fazit ziehen, zusammenfassen	so, all in all

Grammatik:

- if-Sätze: If you ask me, I'd choose Munich. / If you were in Munich you could explore the city. / If you had a couple of days free, you could easily get on a train and visit me!

- sonstige Nebensätze: … whereas on a farm you might often be on your own … / … because you're an outside person. / do the outside activities that you love / … when you come to Germany

- Verneinungen: your German wouldn't improve very much / the animals won't talk to you / don't forget about your free time

- Fragesatz: Does this help you?

- gesteigertes Adjektiv: more difficult

- Adverb: easily

- Modalverben: 'd/would(n't), might, could, can

- present perfect progressive: I've been thinking

- future: the animals won't talk to you / I hope we'll be able to meet

Wortschatz:

1 improve · **2** exhausting · **3** awful · **4** chat · **5** a couple of · **6** tons of

Schritt 3: Jetzt bist du dran!

Lösungsbeispiel:

Hi Amelia

Many thanks for your email. You ask me about the plans for the new airport, and that isn't easy to answer!

On the one hand, I'm worried about the environment (aspect **1** mentioned). The planes will make a lot of noise, especially at night. (included) I'm concerned, too, that our air will be polluted (elaborated) – it's bad enough with the smoke from the factories! (fully elaborated)

What's more, lots of cars and lorries will need to come to the airport. (aspect **2** mentioned) It's true that they are planning to build some new roads (included), but the result could still be that we get lots more traffic through our village. (elaborated) And more traffic will contribute to the noise and pollution. (fully elaborated)

On the other hand, many people are in favour of the airport because it will create new jobs (aspect **3** mentioned) – both long-term employment and holiday jobs for young people. (included) That would be good because it isn't easy for young people to find work here (elaborated). And if people have more money, our community will profit, too. (fully elaborated)

And of course many people like the idea of a new airport because it will make it easier for them to fly to different places. (aspect **4** mentioned) I could be in, say, Glasgow, in two hours! (included) So be careful: I'll maybe come and see you in Scotland every weekend! (elaborated)

So it's difficult to decide! But all in all I think we should welcome new opportunities, so I think the airport will be a good thing.

Best wishes from Germany!

Ben (244 words)

Formal emails or letters

Formelle E-Mails oder Briefe		
	Name des Empfängers bekannt	Name des Empfängers unbekannt
Anrede	Dear Mr/Mrs/Ms (+ name)	Dear Sir/Madam
Schluss	Yours sincerely,	Yours faithfully,

Langformen: I will be away in August. · I am in my last year at school. · I have worked in this cafe since June. · I do not mind working at weekends.

Beispiel 1: Beschwerdebrief

Schritt 1 und 2 (Inhalt, Aufbau und Zusammenhang):

Dear Sir or Madam

I ordered a phone from your online shop on Friday 3rd May. But there have been a few problems.

First, your website promised that deliveries (aspect **1** mentioned) would take a maximum of three days (included), so I was very disappointed when it had not arrived a week later. (elaborated) The short delivery was one of the reasons why I ordered the phone from your shop. (fully elaborated).

I therefore phoned your customer service to find out what was happening. (aspect **3** mentioned) I had to wait a long time before anybody answered the phone (included), and then the assistant I spoke to could not find my order. (elaborated) He did not apologize, but he made a new order. (fully elaborated)

The phone finally arrived at the end of June, but unfortunately it did not work (aspect **2** mentioned). Not only was the front broken (included), but the charger was missing too. (elaborated) As a result, I have been unable to keep in touch with my friends. (fully elaborated)

Naturally I am very unhappy with this service.

Please now send me a new phone. (aspect **4** mentioned) When I have received it, I will then return the broken phone that you sent me. (included) If I do not receive a new phone by the end of this month, I will explain the whole story in an online review. (elaborated)

Many thanks for your cooperation.

Yours faithfully,

Callum Spencer (214 words)

Grammatik:

- past progressive: what was happening
- past perfect: it had not arrived
- future: I will explain
- indirekte Rede: Your website promised that deliveries would take …
- Relativsatz (ohne Relativpronomen): the assistant I spoke to
- if-Satz: If I do not receive a new phone by the end of this month, I will explain …
- sonstiger Nebensatz: When I have received it, I will then …
- Verneinung: the phone did not work

Schritt 3:

Dear Ms Turner

I stayed in your hotel from 1st to 5th May. But I was very unhappy with my room.

To begin with, the bathroom was dirty.

Then, there weren't any towels.

What's more, it was very noisy because people were drinking in front of the hotel all night.

As a result, I didn't get any sleep.

And finally, your website promised a view of the sea, but I couldn't see the sea.

So now I wish to claim compensation for my stay in your hotel.

I look forward to hearing from you soon.

Yours sincerely,
Zoe Smith

Schritt 4: Jetzt bist du dran!

Lösungsbeispiel:

Dear Sir or Madam

On Thursday 26th March my parents and I had lunch in your restaurant next to Victoria Station. I must tell you that we were not satisfied with our experience.

To begin with, the food was very disappointing. (aspect **1** mentioned) My mother's meat was not properly cooked (included). And not only were my potatoes still partly frozen (elaborated), but my steak was as hard as a piece of wood. (fully elaborated)

Moreover, the service was terrible. (aspect **2** mentioned) My father had ordered fish, but the waiter brought sausages. (included) When my father explained, the waiter took the sausages away, but still did not bring the fish (elaborated). Finally, when we wanted to complain to the manager, we were told that she was busy. (fully elaborated)

To make things even worse, the other guests were extremely rude. (aspect **3** mentioned) For example, a woman dropped her glass close to our table and did not even apologize. (included) Shortly afterwards, a man started yelling and the waiters did not do anything to stop him. (elaborated) Is this a way to run a restaurant? (fully elaborated)

So now we would like to claim compensation for the cost of the meal. (aspect **4** mentioned) We paid £ 80 for it. (included) I am sure you will agree that this is not acceptable. (elaborated)

Yours faithfully

Rosa Schröder (202 words)

Beispiel 2: Bewerbungsschreiben

Schritt 1:

Dear Sir or Madam

I read your advert online and I would like to apply for the job of assistant to help in your cafe this summer.

I would love to work in a cafe because I really enjoy having contact with people. What's more, English is my favourite lesson at school, and a summer job in your cafe would give me the chance to improve my English.

As you will see from my CV, I already have some experience because last year I worked in a cafe in Munich. After working in the kitchen for one week, I was given work with the customers. My responsibilities included taking orders, serving customers and clearing the tables. As a result, I am sure that I have the skills that I will need in your cafe.

As far as my personal qualities are concerned, I am honest, reliable and hard-working. I love the interaction with people, but on the other hand I know that the time for talking is limited.

May I please ask you what the pay rate is and whether there is the possibility of accomodation at the cafe? Also, I can only start as from the 1st July. Is this acceptable to you?

I look forward to hearing from you soon.

Yours faithfully,
Daniel Holzberg

Schritt 2:
personal qualities: honest, reliable, hard-working, friendly, polite, team player, organizational skills, confident, enthusiastic, communication skills, social skills, energetic, punctual, flexible, ...

work experience: assistant, part-time, weekend job, summer camp, summer job, first-aid training, voluntary work, member of school council, training, trainee, instructor, basic knowledge, apprenticeship, ...

application words: CV, advert, pay (rate), references, education, skills, qualities, enclose, include, apply, responsibilities, earn, strength, work experience, study, working hours, career, qualification, shift work, requirement, certificate, application form, job interview, available, ...

Schritt 3:

Lösungsbeispiel:

Dear Sir / Madam

I read your advert on my TS (telepathy screen) and I am writing by telepathy to apply for the job.

I think I would be very suitable for the job (aspect **1** mentioned) because I have been interested in robots from a young age (included). While my classmates were wasting their time doing sports, I spent all my time reading robot manuals. (elaborated) There can be few students who know more about robots than I do. (fully elaborated)

I also have valuable experience of working on robots. (aspect **2** mentioned) My parents do not understand robots, so they always ask me for help when a robot stops working. (included) Last week, for example, when our toilet cleaning robot went on strike, I was able to repair it without having to contact the URCC (Universal Robot Care Centre). (elaborated) What's more, I have worked as a babysitter for many years, so I know how to take care of the little ones. (fully elaborated)

As regards my personal qualities (aspect **3** mentioned) I am not only reliable and caring, but also very communicative. (included) This would surely be very useful for showing school groups around the robot station. (elaborated) Finally, I am a hardworking and efficient person and do not mind getting my hands dirty or cleaning after little robots. (fully elaborated)

May I also ask you a couple of questions about the work? (aspect **4** mentioned) Do you offer accommodation for fulltime volunteers? (included) And who are the experts I would be assisting? (elaborated)

Yours faithfully,
R2D2 Skywalker (235 words)

Articles

Lösungsbeispiel:

In May last year I was one of 15 lucky students from our class who spent a week in our partner school in York. (aspect **1** mentioned) We not only had lessons, but also went on trips to places near York. (included) I really enjoyed rock-climbing in the Pennines (elaborated) and the best trip of all was the visit to Whitby, where we played basketball on the beach. (fully elaborated)

In return we will be visited by 15 British students at the end of June, (aspect **2** mentioned) and some of us have begun to put together a programme for them. (included) We have, for example, organized a tour of the castle, and we will all go bowling too. (elaborated) Moreover, if we're lucky with the weather, we'll have a barbecue. (fully elaborated)

The issue of accommodation was not an easy one, (aspect **3** mentioned) because the British students were a bit scared of staying in German-speaking families. (included) They have only had German for one year, so they were worried that they wouldn't understand anything. (elaborated) But we managed to find families with somebody who could speak English, so now everybody is happy. (fully elaborated)

May I finally ask for help when the British students arrive? (aspect **4** mentioned) Please help them if they get lost in our school (included) Do you have time to come and welcome them at the station? (elaborated) We'll be delighted to hear from you. Thank you! (fully elaborated)

(217 words)

Blogs

Tipp:

nice: fantastic, special, amazing, awesome, fascinating, unique, absolutely incredible, one of the most beautiful places I've ever seen, ...

not nice: disappointing, awful, really bad, appalling, dreadful, terrible, a complete waste of time, nothing to write home about, a real let-down, ...

Lösungsbeispiel:

After checking out of our hostel in Krakow we took the train to Prague. (aspect **1** mentioned) What an amazingly awesome city! (included) We joined thousands of tourists as they strolled across the Charles Bridge. (elaborated) And we came back to the bridge in the evening because we wanted to see the castle lit up against the night sky. (fully elaborated)

Strange to think it's the last evening of our trip! (aspect **2** mentioned) Among our many highlights was meeting Maria and swimming together in Croatia. (included) I don't think I've ever met anyone who was so spontaneously friendly. (elaborated) But this evening was certainly a highlight too, because the atmosphere on the bridge was absolutely incredible. So many young people, and such great music! (fully elaborated)

This journey with Karl has not always been easy, but it's been one of the best things I've ever done. (aspect **3** mentioned) I've learned to agree to go and see things that I myself would never have chosen. (included) As a result I've seen lots of fascinating places that I'd never heard of before. (elaborated)

When we leave Prague tomorrow morning, we'll be on our final journey of this holiday. (aspect **4** mentioned) Of course, I'm really looking forward to seeing everybody at home, (included) and I'll be happy to sleep in my own bed again. (elaborated) On the other hand I'll miss Karl, who has been a good companion. And I'll miss the excitement of discovering new places every day! (fully elaborated)

(227 words)

Stories

Tipp:

linking phrases and time adverbials: then, after that, suddenly, at once, after leaving the house, before arriving at the station, following this conversation, on the next afternoon, later that day, the following week, the morning was nearly over when, ...

person: calm, nervous, silly, serious, tall, good-looking, confident, reliable, honest, funny, bad-tempered, ...

feelings: happy, sad, jealous, proud, afraid, angry, bored, shy, excited, top of the world, ...

Lösungsbeispiel:

As it was Dana's first day at work in the clothes shop, she was feeling pretty nervous. (aspect **1** mentioned) Would she make a good impression, she wondered? (included) And what should she do if a customer asked her something she didn't know? (elaborated) Dana tried to concentrate on the music playing in the shop. Luckily, it was by her favourite music star, Max Kingdom. (fully elaborated)

The morning shift was nearly over, and everything had gone well, when suddenly Dana dropped a box of new shirts. (aspect **2** mentioned) They went all over the floor. (included) Some of them even fell onto the carpet near the entrance door, which was wet from the customers' shoes. (elaborated) Dana at once began to pick up the shirts, hoping that they had not got dirty. (fully elaborated)

She was therefore on her hands and knees when the door opened and a new customer walked in. (aspect **3** mentioned) Dana looked up in order to apologize – and that's when she had the shock of her life. (included) For the customer wasn't just any old customer. It was Max Kingdom himself! (elaborated)

"Well, good morning," said Max pleasantly, and smiled. "Have you lost something?" (aspect **4** mentioned) At first Dana was too surprised to say anything. (included) Then she said, "Oh, I just dropped these shirts ...". (elaborated) "Oh, I can help you with that," answered Max. And to Dana's enormous surprise, Max knelt down and helped her pick up the shirts. (fully elaborated)

(226 words)

MUSTERPRÜFUNG 1: Part I: Reading ▶ p. 62

TASK 1:
1 true · 2 true · 3 false · 4 not in the text · 5 true · 6 false

TASK 2:
A 5 · B 8 · C 1 · D 9 · E 6 · F 3

TASK 3:
1 / · 2 when · 3 / · 4 As · 5 / · 6 / · 7 for · 8 / · 9 the · 10 / ·
11 are · 12 / · 13 / · 14 have · 15 /

TASK 4:
1 D · 2 B · 3 C · 4 A · 5 B · 6 C

TASK 5:
Hinweis: Andere Formulierungen sind zulässig, solange der inhaltliche Aspekt (im Lösungsbeispiel unterstrichen) korrekt erfasst ist.

1 Wird seit 60 Jahren (6 Tage die Woche) aufgeführt. / Das Stück, das am längsten aufgeführt wird. / Ist das am längsten aufgeführte Theaterstück der Welt. / …

2 Mutter hatte zuvor dieselbe Rolle. / Übernahm die Rolle ihrer Mutter. / …

3 Kritiker waren nicht sehr begeistert, aber Publikum mochte das Stück. / Publikum war begeistert, Kritiker nicht. / Dem Publikum gefiel das Stück besser als den Theaterkritikern. / …

4 Glaubte, es würde höchstens acht Monate laufen. / Erwartete, dass es nicht sehr lange aufgeführt werden würde. / …

5 Publikum wird gebeten, Auflösung/Geheimnis nicht (in sozialen Medien) zu verraten. · Stück ist nicht als Buch oder Film erschienen. / Stück wurde bisher nicht veröffentlicht. / …

MUSTERPRÜFUNG 1: Part II: Use of English ▶ p. 67

TASK 1:
1 entrance/entrances · 2 litter · 3 of course · 4 (to) place / placed ·
5 on their own

TASK 2:

A	B	C	D	E	F
0	2	7	6	4	5

TASK 3:
1 professional · 2 planting · 3 broken · 4 paid · 5 available ·
6 reference

TASK 4:
1 Of course not everyone succeeds in gaining employment.
2 But the advantages of being in work are understood by most people.
3 Employment provides an income as well as a greater sense of self-value.
4 And most people want to leave the house instead of staying at home all day.

TASK 5:
1 there · 2 more difficult · 3 spectacularly · 4 travelling ·
5 needed · 6 was told · 7 like · 8 best · 9 can be imagined ·
10 course

MUSTERPRÜFUNG 1: Part III: Guided Writing ▶ p. 70

TASK A:

Lösungsbeispiel:

Hi, I hope you enjoy reading my blog!

I live in a pod on the three hundredth floor (aspect 1 mentioned). To save space my sleeping compartment is under my sister's (included). Before I bought it, I had had to eat real food, but now energy is pumped into me while I sleep (elaborated). The sleeping compartments give us more space in the pod for exercising (fully elaborated).

Every morning I fly to the landing pad at school (aspect 2 mentioned). The day's lessons are communicated to our brains in an hour's 'education shower' (included). I then spend most of the rest of the day exploring new countries (elaborated). I travel at the speed of thought, so I can visit several countries each day (fully elaborated).

Weekends are more boring than weekdays (aspect 3 mentioned) because since 2120 young people have had to do community work at weekends (included). My task is to help older people who don't understand robots (elaborated). It's less fun than teaching children how to walk, but it gives me some free time on Sunday (fully elaborated).

My parents are useless with robots, and were stuck when our cleaning robot stopped working this week (aspect 4 mentioned). Just imagine, my dad began to hoover the living room himself! (included) Luckily I was able to repair the robot, because it's inhuman to clean your home yourself! (elaborated)

Tomorrow I'll write about my friends. Read on!

(213 words)

TASK B:

Lösungsbeispiel:

Dear Sir/Madam

I read your advert at the post office and I am writing to apply for the job.

I have always been interested in helping older people (aspect 1 mentioned) because I am fascinated by the stories that they tell (included). I am hoping to be a social worker when I leave school (elaborated) and working in the Day Centre would give me useful experience (fully elaborated).

I think I would be suitable for the job (aspect 2 mentioned) because I have experience of helping my grandad, who is 85 (included). I often get his meals ready and we chat eating (elaborated). As a result, I know how important it is to give older people time to talk (fully elaborated).

As regards my personal qualities (aspect **3** mentioned) I am reliable and caring, and very patient when people need time to do simple things (included). I do not mind getting my hands dirty or cleaning after people (elaborated). And of course I have a clean record as far as the police files are concerned (fully elaborated).

May I also ask you a couple of questions about the work? (aspect **4** mentioned) What is the rate of pay for a person under 21? (included) And I have already booked a holiday from 20th to 27th June – is that OK? (elaborated)

I look forward to hearing from you.

Yours faithfully

Lucian Schneider (202 words)

MUSTERPRÜFUNG 1: Listening Test ▶ p. 70

TASK 1:
A 3 · B / · C 1 · D 5 · E / · F 2 · G / · H 4

TASK 2:
1 D · 2 B · 3 D · 4 C

TASK 3:
dizzy → busy · drumming → coming · slides → glides · place → space · new → view

TASK 4:

The role of cricket in India		
A comparison between cricket and basketball:		
	Cricket:	Basketball:
Number of countries in the World Cup:	14	24
Number of fans worldwide:	2.5 billion	400 million
Reasons why cricket has so many fans:		
1) Cricket is very popular in India.		
2) India has a very large / huge population.		
What people in other countries know about cricket:		
– Games last five days / are very long / … – Players don't move much / a lot. / … – Players wear long white trousers. / … (2 von 3 möglichen Aspekten)		
New features in Twenty20 Cricket:		
1) Games are shorter.		
2) Games are more exciting.		

TASK 5:

1 The position of the islands of St Kilda is special because they are … alone in the Atlantic. / so far from the nearest land. / 160 km from the west coast of Scotland. / …

2 Liz and Richard went there because they wanted to see … every UNESCO site in Britain.

3 It wasn't easy to get to St Kilda because … the weather was so bad. / the conditions weren't right. / …

4 What makes the St Kilda mice and sheep so special is that … they only exist there. / they don't exist anywhere else in the world. / …

5 The St Kildans survived by … catching (sea) birds and farming.

6 The rocks are so steep that the people couldn't keep boats and so they … couldn't catch fish. / couldn't go fishing. / …

7 The population of St Kilda fell because the young left and … men / many died in the First World War.

8 On St Kilda today you see a museum and … ruins of houses / an old street. / some cottages. / …

MUSTERPRÜFUNG 2: Part I: Reading ▶ p. 74

TASK 1:
A 6 · B 8 · C 4 · D 7 · E 1 · F 3

TASK 2:
1 false · 2 true · 3 false · 4 not in the text · 5 false · 6 true · 7 true · 8 true · 9 false · 10 not in the text

TASK 3:
1 well · 2 it · 3 / · 4 at · 5 so · 6 / · 7 has · 8 / · 9 if · 10 been

TASK 4:
Hinweis: Andere Formulierungen sind zulässig, solange der inhaltliche Aspekt (im Lösungsbeispiel unterstrichen) korrekt erfasst ist.

1 Impfung/Tabletten/Schutz gegen Malaria wird/werden überprüft/gecheckt. · Gebühr muss bezahlt werden.

2 mit dem eigenen Wagen/Auto · in einer Gruppe / mit anderen Besuchern in der Begleitung eines Rangers

3 die größte Vielfalt der Welt / mehr unterschiedliche Tiere als in allen anderen Tierparks der Welt / größte Bandbreite an Tieren in aller Welt

4 Laden/Geschäft/Shop, Erste Hilfe, Gemeinschaftsküchen/ Kochmöglichkeit, Tankstelle

5 Man braucht eine Genehmigung/Erlaubnis.

MUSTERPRÜFUNG 2: Part II: Use of English ▶ p. 77

TASK 1:
1 (to) forbid / forbidden · 2 inescapable · 3 frequently ·
4 the majority of · 5 (to) improve / improved

TASK 2:
put down: hier: unterdrücken, niederschlagen · make up: hier:
etw. ausmachen, bilden · get on: hier: auskommen

TASK 3:
1 dangerously · 2 reduction · 3 government · 4 citizens ·
5 achieved · 6 Luckily · 7 politicians

TASK 4:
1 Not many South Africans today are as famous as Elon Musk.

2 Elon Musk invests both in rockets and (in) / in both rockets
and electric cars.

3 Electric cars were made popular by Elon Musk.

4 If his dreams are realized, he will affect how we live, too.

TASK 5:
1 these · 2 largest · 3 from · 4 is spoken · 5 third · 6 who ·
7 found · 8 surprisingly · 9 were planted · 10 over/around

MUSTERPRÜFUNG 2: Part III: Guided Writing ▶ p. 80

TASK A:
Lösungsbeispiel:

The country that I would most like to visit is New Zealand
(aspect 1 mentioned). The two islands on the other side of the
world offer spectacular landscapes (included). They are safe
from tropical diseases (elaborated) and it's easy to find your way
around because everybody speaks English (fully elaborated).

The place that I dream of most is Fjordland (aspect 2 mentioned),
which is in the south of South Island (included). Steep mountains rise from fjords that look a bit like Norway (elaborated).
This region was filmed in *The Lord of the Rings* and I have been
fascinated by it ever since seeing the film (fully elaborated).

If I had enough money, I would go trekking in the mountains
(aspect 3 mentioned). It is a dangerous activity if you do it on
your own (included), but there are organized tours with experi-
enced guides who can take you to the most amazing places
(elaborated). You camp outside, and see the stars perfectly,
because there are no city lights nearby (fully elaborated).

But flights to New Zealand are unfortunately very expensive
(aspect 4 mentioned) and the guided tour would be another
very large cost (included). But, having just returned from a wonderful two-week trip to Scotland, my bank account is empty.
(elaborated) So memories of Scotland will have to take the
place of dreams of New Zealand. (fully elaborated)

(200 words)

TASK B:

Lösungsbeispiel:

Dear Sir or Madam

In May my parents and I decided on a holiday in South Africa and
booked two nights in your hotel.

We thought that it would be convenient because you claim it is
near the airport. (aspect 1 mentioned) We expected a large
family room with a bathroom (included) and free access to the
pool and gym (elaborated). And we looked forward to what your
advert called authentic South African cuisine. (fully elaborated)

We stayed in your hotel from 13th to 15th August and were very
disappointed. (aspect 2 mentioned) Instead of a family room,
we were given three separate single rooms. (included) None
of them had its own bathroom as your advert had promised
(elaborated). And the food in the restaurant was the same as
any food in a cheap restaurant in Germany. (fully elaborated)

To make things even worse, the hotel staff were not helpful
when we complained. (aspect 3 mentioned) We were not
offered alternative rooms. (included) In fact we were not even
given an apology. (elaborated) Is this a way to run a hotel?
(fully elaborated)

So now we would like to claim compensation for the cost of our
stay. (aspect 4 mentioned) We paid 3000 rand for it. (included)
I am sure you will agree that at least half of this should be paid
back to us. (elaborated)

Yours faithfully

Lotte Mandelbaum

(202 words)

MUSTERPRÜFUNG 2: Listening Test ▶ p. 81

TASK 1:
A 3 · B / · C 5 · D / · E 1 · F / · G 2 · H 4

TASK 2:
1 B · 2 C · 3 A · 4 C

TASK 3:
chilly → hilly · grounds → towns · landing → standing ·
queue → grew · plenty → many · Blue → New

TASK 4:

Two fantastic cycle races	
What was special about the 2014 Tour de France:	started in Yorkshire / came to Yorkshire (for the first time)
How long does the race take?	
Tour de France:	3 weeks
Tour de Yorkshire:	3 days
How people in Yorkshire reacted to the Tour de France (2 examples):	
– pubs changed their names / took French names – butchers made pies in the shape of bicycles – they went wild / were enthusiastic – celebrated on the street / had street parties – put yellow bicycles on pavement or in front garden (2 von mehreren möglichen Aspekten)	
The meaning of yellow in the Tour de France:	winner of each stage wears yellow / it's the official colour (of the Tour de France)
Why some cyclists are surprised by the roads in Yorkshire (2 examples):	
– they are steep – they are narrow – they are twisty (2 von 3 möglichen Aspekten)	

TASK 5:

1 Jack slept badly because … he slept on the ground. / the ground was hard. / the ground wasn't exactly soft. / …

2 The reporter is surprised because Katie … is only wearing one boot. / has only one boot. / has a plastic bag on her foot. / is wearing a plastic bag. / …

3 The aim of the D of E Award is to enable young people … to have adventures in the country. / to experience adventure out in the countryside. / …

4 The expedition at Silver Level lasts … three days and two nights.

5 Participants are allowed to bring a smartphone, but … they can only use it for taking photos or in an emergency. / they are not allowed to use a hiking app or GPS. / no more than one smartphone for the whole group. / they have to use a map or compass to find their way. / …

6 When Katie and Jack got lost they … walked around the same field twice / two times / again.

7 They are now waiting because … the other members of their group are behind them. / they have to let the others catch up. / they are faster than their friends. /…

Die Tonaufnahmen (MP3-Dateien) und die Hörtexte findest du online unter www.scook.de/bayern.
Deinen persönlichen Zugangscode findest du auf Seite 1 deines Abschlussprüfungstrainers.

Track	Kapitel	Titel	Seite
1	Training Section	Listening: Radio ads	15
2	Training Section	Listening: A visit to Krakow	16
3	Training Section	Listening: A tourist attraction in Brighton (Part 1)	17
4	Training Section	Listening: Bob Marley	18
5	Training Section	Listening: A guided tour of Bo-Kaap	19
6	Training Section	Listening: The Niagara Falls (Part 1)	20
7	Training Section	Listening: The Niagara Falls (Part 2)	21
8	Training Section	Listening: The Niagara Falls (Part 3)	21
9	Musterprüfung 1	Listening, Task 1: Reasons for speaking	70
10	Musterprüfung 1	Listening, Task 2: My foreign language experience	71
11	Musterprüfung 1	Listening, Task 3: A tourist attraction in Brighton (Part 2)	72
12	Musterprüfung 1	Listening, Task 4: Cricket in India	72
13	Musterprüfung 1	Listening, Task 5: St Kilda – a World Heritage site	73
14	Musterprüfung 2	Listening, Task 1: Jobs in Canada	81
15	Musterprüfung 2	Listening, Task 2: Calgary's Skyways	81
16	Musterprüfung 2	Listening, Task 3: A presentation about Wales	82
17	Musterprüfung 2	Listening, Task 4: Two fantastic cycle races	83
18	Musterprüfung 2	Listening, Task 5: The D of E expedition	84
19	Urheberrechtserklärung		

Studio: Clarity Studio Berlin

Regie und Aufnahmeleitung: Christian Schmitz

Tontechnik: Hüseyin Dönertaş, Christian Marx

Written Test, Part III: Guided Writing (gelenktes Schreiben)

Die schriftliche Prüfung *(Written Test)* besteht aus drei Teilen:
- Part I: Leseverstehen *(Reading)*
- Part II: Wortschatz und Grammatik *(Use of English)*
- **Part III: gelenktes Schreiben** *(Guided Writing)*

Für diese drei schriftlichen Prüfungsteile hast du insgesamt 105 Minuten Zeit. Du kannst dir diese Zeit selbst einteilen. Plane also genügend Zeit für jeden Teil ein und bedenke dabei, dass du am Ende auch noch Zeit zum Korrekturlesen benötigst.

1. Ablauf beim Schreiben

Im dritten Teil der schriftlichen Prüfung schreibst du selbst einen längeren Text von ca. 200 Wörtern. Hierfür erhältst du zwei Aufgaben zur Auswahl – meist einen etwas stärker gelenkten Schreibauftrag, der eine E-Mail, eine Annonce oder Ähnliches zur Grundlage hat, und einen Schreibauftrag, den du stärker mit eigener Fantasie füllen kannst.

Die Textsorten, die du produzieren sollst, sind vielfältig: So musst du z. B. ein Bewerbungsschreiben, eine persönliche oder formelle E-Mail, eine Kurzgeschichte mit vorgegebenem Anfang, einen Blog, Artikel, Beschwerdebrief etc. schreiben. In jedem Fall sind vier inhaltliche Aspekte *(prompts)* vorgegeben, die in deiner Lösung enthalten sein müssen.

Wörterbücher oder andere Hilfsmittel sind in der Prüfung nicht erlaubt.

2. Bewertung beim Schreiben

Bei *Guided Writing* kannst du (wie bei allen anderen Prüfungsteilen) 30 Punkte erreichen. Dieser Prüfungsteil macht also 20% der Gesamtnote aus.

Die Bewertungskriterien
Die 30 Punkte verteilen sich auf folgende Kriterien:
- Inhalt *(task achievement)*: maximal 7 Punkte
- Aufbau und Zusammenhang *(coherence and cohesion)*: maximal 7 Punkte
- Grammatik *(grammar)*: maximal 7 Punkte
- Wortschatz *(vocabulary)*: maximal 7 Punkte
- Gesamteindruck *(impression of general quality)*: maximal 2 Punkte

> **Tipp**
>
> Weitere Informationen zur Bewertung findest du hier: https://www.isb.bayern.de/schulartspezifisches/leistungserhebungen/abschlusspruefungen-realschule/englisch/begleitmaterialien/

Inhalt *(task achievement)*
Hier geht es darum, wie gut du die vier Aspekte der Aufgabenstellung *(prompts)* ausgearbeitet hast. Um die volle Punktzahl zu erhalten, musst du in deinem Text alle vier Aspekte ansprechen und näher ausführen:
- Benenne direkt oder indirekt (z.B. mithilfe eines *topic sentence*) den jeweiligen Aspekt *(prompt)*.
- Führe anschließend diesen Aspekt weiter aus. Hierfür gibt es im Bewertungsbogen deines Prüfers oder deiner Prüferin drei Stufen:
  - **voll ausgearbeitet** *(fully elaborated)*: Du führst **drei** Gedanken/Ideen/Unterpunkte/Details aus.
  - **ausgearbeitet** *(elaborated)*: Du führst **zwei** Gedanken/Ideen/Unterpunkte/Details aus.
  - **inbegriffen** *(included)*: Du führst **einen** Gedanken/Idee/Unterpunkt/Detail aus.
- So verfährst du mit allen vier Aspekten.

In Punkten drückt sich das so aus:

Punkte	Deine Leistung im Bereich Inhalt *(task achievement)*
7	Du hast alle vier Aspekte angesprochen und mindestens drei davon **voll ausgearbeitet**.
6	Deine Leistung und deine Punktzahl liegen zwischen 5 und 7.
5	Du hast alle vier Aspekte angesprochen und mindestens drei davon **ausgearbeitet**.
4	Deine Leistung und deine Punktzahl liegen zwischen 3 und 5.
3	Du hast mindestens drei Aspekte angesprochen und zwei davon **ausgearbeitet**.
2	Deine Leistung und deine Punktzahl liegen zwischen 1 und 3.
1	Du hast mehrere Aspekte ausgelassen und den angesprochenen Aspekt nicht weiter ausgeführt.
0	Du hast viel zu wenig geschrieben oder das Thema völlig verfehlt.

Aufbau und Zusammenhang *(coherence & cohesion)*

Hier geht es darum, ob dein Text logisch aufgebaut und deine Sätze sinnvoll und abwechslungsreich miteinander verknüpft sind (Stichwort *linking words*). Die Reihenfolge, in der du die vier Aspekte „abarbeitest", darf von der Reihenfolge in der Arbeitsanweisung abweichen, solange der Textaufbau insgesamt logisch ist.

Grammatik *(grammar)*

In diesem Bereich zählen sowohl die Vielfalt *(range)* als auch die Korrektheit *(accuracy)* der von dir verwendeten grammatischen Strukturen. Du kannst auch mit einigen kleineren Fehlern noch die volle Punktzahl erreichen, wenn man erkennt, dass du verschiedene (auch komplexere) Strukturen sinnvoll und weitgehend korrekt einsetzt.

Wortschatz *(vocabulary)*

Hier geht es ebenfalls um Vielfalt *(range)* und Korrektheit *(accuracy)* deines Wortschatzes. Auch hier sind einige kleinere Fehler erlaubt, solange du zeigst, dass du dich abwechslungsreich und treffend ausdrücken kannst.

Gesamteindruck *(impression of general quality)*

Die Prüferin oder der Prüfer kann zwei weitere Punkte für den Gesamteindruck vergeben. Hierzu zählt, ob Form und Stil deines Textes angemessen sind und ob dein Text (z.B. ein Beschwerdebrief oder ein Bewerbungsschreiben) seinen Zweck erfüllt.

Die Textlänge

Du sollst ungefähr 200 Wörter schreiben. Ist dein Text deutlich kürzer als 200 Wörter, so schlägt sich das negativ bei den Bewertungskriterien (s.o.) nieder. Schreibst du weniger als 140 Wörter, so kannst du bei den 7-Punkte-Kriterien nicht mehr als 5 Punkte bekommen. Schreibst du weniger als 100 Wörter, so kannst du nicht mehr als 3 Punkte pro Kriterium bekommen. Und schreibst du sogar weniger als 70 Wörter, so gibt es höchstens einen Punkt für jedes Kriterium. Für zu lange Texte gibt es dagegen keinen automatischen Punktabzug.

Tipp

Zähle regelmäßig die Wörter deiner Texte, auch bei Hausaufgaben. So bekommst du ein Gefühl für die Länge!

3. Typische Aufgabenformate

In diesem Kapitel lernst du die typischen Aufgabenformate kennen, die dich bei der Abschlussprüfung im Bereich Schreiben erwarten. Die Tipp-Kästen enthalten nützliche Hinweise und Hilfen.

Personal emails

Das vielleicht häufigste Aufgabenformat beim *Guided Writing* ist das Verfassen einer persönlichen E-Mail. Es kann dir eine E-Mail vorgegeben werden, die du beantworten sollst, oder eine Situation oder ein Thema, zu dem du dich äußern sollst. Es kann im Rahmen einer persönlichen E-Mail auch eine Meinungsäußerung von dir verlangt werden. In jedem Fall erhältst du vier Aspekte, die du erwähnen und ausarbeiten musst. Außerdem wird von dir erwartet, dass du einen passenden Anfang und ein passendes Ende für deine E-Mail findest.

Die Prüfungsaufgabe kann zum Beispiel so aussehen:

Your friend Danny wants to improve his German during the summer and has applied for summer jobs in Germany. He has sent you the following email:

> Hi there,
>
> As you know, I applied for six different jobs, and two places have offered me work in August! The first is a cafe in the centre of Munich – I can work in their kitchens. And the second job is working in the fields of a farm out in the country, about ten kilometres from Regensburg. So I wanted to ask you: which job would be better? Which one should I accept?
> Say hi to the family.
> Danny

Answer Danny's email. In your mail, include the following aspects:
- opportunity to speak German
- type of work
- location
- leisure time

Find a suitable beginning and ending. **Write about 200 words.**

Schritt 1: Lies die Arbeitsanweisung genau durch und mache dir klar, was für eine Art E-Mail du schreiben sollst. Dein Schreiben muss zum Empfänger passen – hier ist das ein Freund. Dein Stil kann also locker sein, auch bei Anrede und Schluss. Fülle zur Wiederholung folgende Tabelle aus:

Persönliche E-Mails	
Anrede	*Dear (+name),*
Schluss	*Bye for now,*

Schritt 2: Schau dir nun das Lösungsbeispiel auf Seite 46 an. Du kannst daran sehen, wie du in allen Bewertungskriterien Punkte gewinnen kannst.

Dear Danny

Thanks for your mail – that's awesome news! I've been thinking a lot about your question.

Munich or a Bavarian farm – if you ask me, I'd choose Munich! Think of all the exciting shops, the cinemas, the cafes. A farm, however, is not so much different from a farm in England ...

What's more, your aim was to improve your German. In Munich you would meet tons of people, whereas on a farm you might often be on your own and so it could be more difficult for you to practise your German. As a result, your German wouldn't improve very much.

On the other hand, farm work would probably be more your kind of thing because you're an outside person. And you're really good with animals! But then again, the animals won't talk to you ☺ and farm work can be exhausting, especially in awful weather!

And finally, don't forget about your free time. If you were in Munich you could explore the city and chat with people. Besides, if you had a couple of days free, you could easily get on a train and visit me! Or else you could spend the weekend in the mountains and do the outside activities that you love.

So all in all I would recommend the job in town. Does this help you? Good luck, and I hope we'll be able to meet when you come to Germany!

Love,
Nurit

Inhalt *(task achievement)*
Hier geht es vor allem um das „Abarbeiten" der vier Aspekte *(prompts)*. Markiere die Sätze
- zu Sprachgelegenheiten (Aspekt 1) gelb
- zu den konkreten Tätigkeiten (Aspekt 2) grün
- zum Ort (Aspekt 3) rot
- zu den Freizeitmöglichkeiten (Aspekt 4) blau.

> **Tipp**
> Alle vier Aspekte müssen bearbeitet werden, aber nicht unbedingt in der Reihenfolge der Arbeitsanweisung.

Prüfe nun:
- Sind alle vier Aspekte der Aufgabenstellung erwähnt?
- Wieviele Gedanken/Ideen/Unterpunkte/Details sind zu den vier Aspekten jeweils ausgearbeitet?
- Wieviele Punkte hat der Text im Bereich Inhalt deiner Meinung nach also verdient? (Seite 44)

Aufbau und Zusammenhang *(coherence & cohesion)*
Überprüfe nun, ob das Lösungsbeispiel logisch aufgebaut ist und die Sätze sinnvoll und abwechslungsreich miteinander verknüpft sind. Verbindungswörter spielen hier eine entscheidende Rolle. Notiere die Verbindungswörter aus dem Text:

> **Tipp**
> Verbindungswörter *(linking words)* verbinden Satzteile oder Sätze miteinander. Sie helfen dir, Gedanken zu ordnen, Gründe anzugeben, Sachverhalte gegenüberzustellen, Schlussfolgerungen zu ziehen etc. Dadurch wird dein Text besser verständlich und abwechslungsreicher.

Verbindungswörter und -phrasen	
Funktion	**Beispiel**
Informationen/Gedanken/... hinzufügen	*what's more,*
Die Reihenfolge verdeutlichen	
Gegenteil/Kontrast ausdrücken	
Begründung/Zweck anführen	
Gedankengänge abschließen	
Ein Fazit ziehen, zusammenfassen	

Grammatik *(grammar)*

Hier geht es um die korrekte Verwendung einer Viel-zahl an (auch komplexen) Strukturen. Finde in der Musterlösung Beispiele für die folgenden Strukturen:

if-Sätze: _____

_____

_____

sonstige Nebensätze: _____

_____

_____

Verneinungen: _____

_____

_____

einen Fragesatz: _____

ein gesteigertes Adjektiv: _____

ein Adverb: _____

Modalverben: _____

komplexere Zeitformen: _____

- *present perfect progressive:* _____

- *future:* _____

Wortschatz *(vocabulary)*
Hier geht es darum, dass du Wörter passend verwendest und richtig schreibst. Zusätzlich gewinnst du aber Punkte für einen breiten Wortschatz. Versuche Wiederholungen zu vermeiden!

Das Lösungsbeispiel auf Seite 46 enthält breiten Wortschatz. Wie wird Folgendes im Text ausgedrückt:

0   That's <u>great</u> news!   *awesome*

1   wouldn't <u>get better</u>   _____

2   farm work can be <u>hard</u>   _____

3   in <u>bad</u> weather   _____

4   <u>talk</u> with people   _____

5   <u>some</u> days free   _____

6   <u>many</u> people   _____

> **Tipp**
>
> Manche Redewendungen lassen sich leicht in anderen Kontexten verwenden.
> Du könntest sie auswendig lernen und sie dann selber verwenden – entweder so, wie sie sind, oder leicht verändert.
> Aus diesem Text zum Beispiel:
>
> - *That's awesome news.*
> - *I've been thinking a lot about your question.*
> - *All in all, I would recommend ...*

> **Tipp**
>
> Adjektive machen sich in den meisten Texten gut. Dein Text liest sich dadurch interessanter. Versuche aber, nicht immer dieselben Adjektive *(nice, great, bad, ...)* zu verwenden, sondern eine größere Bandbreite.

Schritt 3: Jetzt bist du dran!

> There are plans to build a new airport about 10 kilometres from your house. An English friend wants to know if you think it's a good idea.
>
> **Write an email** to your friend and say what you like and what you don't like about the idea of a new airport so close to you.
>
> Include the following aspects:
> - environment
> - traffic
> - employment
> - your own travel
>
> Find a suitable beginning and ending. **Write about 200 words.**

a)
Die vier Aspekte aus der Aufgabenstellung geben dir bereits eine Struktur und mögliche Argumente an die Hand. Deine Aufgabe besteht dann vor allem darin, die Aspekte zu bewerten, zu gewichten und sinnvoll miteinander zu verbinden. Du kannst die folgende Tabelle nutzen, um deine Ideen zu sammeln.

> **Tipp**
>
> Keine Angst, wenn du nicht zu jedem Aspekt drei Unterpunkte findest. Du kannst dann immer noch fünf oder sechs Punkte bekommen!

beginning	*Many thanks ... You ask me ...*	
aspect 1: environment	*worried about the environment*	mentioned
Unterpunkt 1	*noise*	included
Unterpunkt 2	*air pollution*	elaborated
Unterpunkt 3		fully elaborated
aspect 2: traffic		mentioned
Unterpunkt 1		included
Unterpunkt 2		elaborated
Unterpunkt 3		fully elaborated
aspect 3: jobs		mentioned
Unterpunkt 1		included
Unterpunkt 2		elaborated
Unterpunkt 3		fully elaborated
aspect 4: own travel		mentioned
Unterpunkt 1		included
Unterpunkt 2		elaborated
Unterpunkt 3		fully elaborated
ending		

b) In dieser Aufgabe ist deine Meinung gefragt. Zu welchem Ergebnis kommst du? Bist du für oder gegen den Flughafen? Auch eine abgewogene Position (einerseits, andererseits) ist in Ordnung.

c) Nun kannst du deinen Text formulieren. Für Meinungsäußerungen gibt es viele nützliche Redewendungen. Nutze auch einige Verbindungswörter aus der Übersicht auf Seite 50.

Stellung nehmen:
In my opinion/view/experience ...
To my mind ...
On the one hand, I (don't) think that ...
On the other hand, ...
I definitely/really (don't) think that ...
Personally, I (don't) think/believe that ...
Many people say that ... / are in favour of ...
However, it's also true that ...
I'm in favour of ... because ...
But in other ways I'm against ...
I agree/disagree with the opinion that ...

Befürchtungen oder Zweifel ausdrücken:
I'm really worried that ...
And in addition, I'm concerned that ...
Another doubt that I have is that ...
I'm not quite sure whether ...

Tipp

Diese Redewendungen sind nur eine kleine Auswahl. Suche weitere Beispiele und schreibe sie auf. Dann kannst du vor der Prüfung eine breite Palette an Redewendungen für die Meinungsäußerung wiederholen. Sie können auch bei der *Speaking*-Prüfung nützlich sein.

Tipp

Vor- und Nachteile von Überlänge:
Wenn du mehr als 200 Wörter schreibst, hast du mehr Möglichkeiten, viele Inhaltspunkte zu sammeln sowie eine Bandbreite an Redewendungen, Verbindungswörtern und grammatischen Strukturen unterzubringen.

Wenn du aber viel zu viel schreibst, hast du weniger Zeit, deinen Text zu überprüfen und ihn zu verbessern. Und in einem langen Text kannst du natürlich auch mehr Fehler machen.

Quantität imponiert – aber nicht auf Kosten der Qualität!

Zugeständnisse machen – und dann Gegenargumente aufführen:
Of course, it's true that ... but ...
Although it's true that ... I still think that ...

Zu einem Ergebnis kommen:
In conclusion, I would say that ...
So all in all I'm against / in favour of ...

Verbindungswörter und -phrasen	
Funktion	**Beispiel**
Informationen / Gedanken / ... hinzufügen	*and, besides, what's more, as well as, furthermore, also, moreover, in addition, not only ... but also, ...*
Die Reihenfolge verdeutlichen	*first – second – third, to begin with, at the beginning, as a start, then, next, before, lastly, finally, at the end, in the end, ...*
Die zeitliche Abfolge verdeutlichen	*afterwards, as soon as, before, meanwhile, then, until, at the same time, after a few hours, ...*
Gegenteil/Kontrast ausdrücken	*but, although, however, whereas, but then again, or else, even though, in contrast, whereas, on the one hand – on the other hand, neither ... nor, in spite of, nevertheless, otherwise, ...*
Begründung/Zweck anführen	*because, as, since, this is why, due to, for this reason, therefore, ...*
Vergleiche anstellen	*in comparison, similarly, ...*
Beispiele anführen	*for example, for instance, to illustrate, that is, namely, such as, ...*
Etwas einräumen	*naturally, of course, yet, still, however, although, nevertheless, in any case, ...*
Gedankengänge abschließen	*as a result, (and) so, therefore, as a consequence, ...*
Ein Fazit ziehen, zusammenfassen	*so, all in all, to sum up, in summary, to conclude, consequently, in conclusion, on the whole, therefore, in brief, summing up, ...*

Schritt 4: Jetzt bist du Prüferin oder Prüfer!
Lies die E-Mail eines Partners oder einer Partnerin und beurteile sie anhand dieser Checkliste:

Tipp
Es ist immer leichter, Fehler bei anderen zu finden. Daher ist es eine sehr gute Übung, fremde Texte zu überprüfen.

Checkliste:	
Hat der Text die geforderte Länge (mindestens 200 Wörter)?	☐
Gibt es einen passenden Anfang und Schluss?	☐
Task achievement: Sind alle vier Aspekte berücksichtigt und ausgearbeitet?	☐
Coherence&cohesion: Enthält der Text eine Bandbreite an sinnvollen Verbindungswörtern?	☐
Grammar: Enthält der Text eine Vielfalt an (auch komplexeren) grammatischen Strukturen?	☐
Vocabulary: Enthält der Text einen angemessenen und breiten Wortschatz in weitgehend korrekter Rechtschreibung?	☐
Impression of general quality: Passt der Stil des Schreibens zum Leser und zur Textsorte?	☐

Entscheide, wie viele Punkte der Text verdient:

• *Task achievement* (maximal 7 Punkte): _____

• *Coherence&cohesion* (maximal 7 Punkte): _____

• *Grammar* (maximal 7 Punkte): _____

• *Vocabulary* (maximal 7 Punkte): _____

• *Impression of general quality*: (maximal 2 Punkte): _____

Formal emails or letters

In der Prüfung können dir auch formelle E-Mails oder Briefe begegnen. Typische Beispiele sind Beschwerdebriefe oder Bewerbungsschreiben. Wieder erhältst du vier Aspekte, die du erwähnen und ausarbeiten musst. Außerdem wird von dir erwartet, dass du einen passenden Anfang und ein passendes Ende findest. Bei formellen E-Mails oder Briefen gibt es jedoch einige Besonderheiten, die du beachten solltest:

Allgemeine Regeln für formelle E-Mails oder Briefe

Bei formellen Schreiben wendest du dich an jemanden, den du nicht oder kaum kennst. Dein Stil sollte daher höflich und sachlich sein. Es gibt einige typische Redewendungen vor allem für die Anrede und den Schluss, die du dir einprägen solltest. Fülle zur Wiederholung folgende Tabelle aus:

Tipp
Schau in dein Englischbuch, falls du diese Wendungen vergessen hast.

Formelle E-Mails oder Briefe		
	Name des Empfängers bekannt	Name des Empfängers unbekannt
Anrede	*Dear Mr/Mrs/Ms (+ name)*	*Dear* _____
Schluss	*Yours* _____	
	Etwas weniger formeller Schluss: *Regards,* *Best wishes,*	

In formellen E-Mails solltest du die Langform der Verben verwenden:

nicht: ~~I'd like to apply for the job.~~   sondern: *I would like to apply for the job.* _____

nicht: ~~I'll be away in August.~~   sondern: _____

nicht: ~~I'm in my last year at school~~.   sondern: _____

nicht: ~~I've worked in this cafe since~~ June.   sondern: _____

nicht: ~~I don't mind working at we~~ekends.   sondern: _____

Beispiel 1: Beschwerdebrief
Die Prüfungsaufgabe kann zum Beispiel so aussehen:

> You ordered a new phone from an online catalogue. Unfortunately, some problems occurred.
>
> Write an **email** and <u>complain</u> about:
> * delivery
> * missing or broken parts
> * service when you phoned
>
> <u>Include:</u> what you expect the company to do
>
> Find a suitable beginning and ending. **Write about 200 words.**

Schritt 1: Lies das folgende Lösungsbeispiel und fülle dabei die Lücken mit Wortschatz aus dem Kasten.

Dear [_____]

I [_____] a phone from your online shop on Friday 3rd May. But there have been

a few problems.

First, your website [_____] that deliveries would take a maximum of three

days, so I was very [_____] when it had not arrived a week later. The short

[_____] was one of the reasons why I ordered the phone from your shop.

I therefore phoned your [_____] to find out what was happening. I had to

wait a long time before anybody answered the phone, and then the assistant I spoke to could not

find my [_____]. He did not [_____], but he made a new order.

The phone finally arrived at the end of June, but unfortunately it did not [_____].

Not only was the front [_____], but the charger was [_____] too.

As a result, I have been unable to keep in touch with my friends.

Naturally I am very [_____] with this service.

Please now send me a new phone. When I have [_____] it, I will then [_____]

the broken phone that you sent me. If I do not receive a new phone by the end of this month, I will

explain the whole story in an [_____].

Many [_____] for your [_____].

Yours [_____],

Callum Spencer

> work • online review • Sir or
> Madam • broken • customer
> service • faithfully • promised •
> ordered • delivery • order •
> cooperation • disappointed •
> return • thanks • missing •
> unhappy • received • apologize

Schritt 2: Analysiere nun das Lösungsbeispiel genauer. So lernst du, wie du selber in der Prüfung mehr Punkte sammeln kannst.

Inhalt *(task achievement)*:
Lies das Lösungsbeispiel gründlich und hake die Inhaltspunkte in der Tabelle ab.

Aufbau und Zusammenhang *(coherence&cohesion)*:
Unterstreiche die Verbindungswörter.

Grammatik *(grammar)*:
Notiere für jede der folgenden Strukturen ein Beispiel aus dem Text:

komplexere Zeitformen:

*   *past progressive:* _____

*   *past perfect:* _____

*   *future:* _____

Indirekte Rede: _____

_____

Relativsatz (ohne Relativpronomen):_____

_____

if-Satz: _____

_____

Sonstiger Nebensatz: _____

_____

Verneinung: _____

_____

beginning	✓	
aspect 1: delivery	✓	mentioned
Unterpunkt 1		included
Unterpunkt 2		elaborated
Unterpunkt 3		fully elaborated
aspect 2: missing/ broken parts		mentioned
Unterpunkt 1		included
Unterpunkt 2		elaborated
Unterpunkt 3		fully elaborated
aspect 3: service		mentioned
Unterpunkt 1		included
Unterpunkt 2		elaborated
Unterpunkt 3		fully elaborated
aspect 4: what to do now		mentioned
Unterpunkt 1		included
Unterpunkt 2		elaborated
Unterpunkt 3		fully elaborated
ending		

Tipp

Versuche, auch komplexere grammatische Strukturen in deinen Text einzubauen, z.B. *participle constructions*, *gerunds*, wörtliche Rede, unterschiedliche Zeitformen, Nebensätze etc.

Wortschatz *(vocabulary)*:
Mit dem Wortschatz hast du dich schon bei Schritt 1 beschäftigt. Hier kannst du dir vier Redewendungen notieren, die bei einem Beschwerdebrief nützlich sein könnten.

Schritt 3: Brauchst du noch etwas Übung mit den Verbindungswörtern? Lies diese kurze Beschwerdemail. Sie enthält keine Verbindungswörter und liest sich daher nicht gut. Verbessere den Text, indem du die Verbindungswörter im Kasten verwendest.

> Then • So now • But •
> As a result • but •
> because • What's more •
> And finally •
> To begin with

Dear Ms Turner

I stayed in your hotel from 1st to 5th May.

I was very unhappy with my room.
The bathroom was dirty.
There weren't any towels.
It was very noisy. People were drinking in front of the hotel all night.
I didn't get any sleep.
Your website promised a view of the sea. I couldn't see the sea.

I wish to claim compensation for my stay in your hotel.

I look forward to hearing from you soon.

Yours sincerely,
Zoe Smith

Schritt 4: Jetzt bist du dran! Lies die Aufgabe und schreibe deine Mail.

> You had lunch in a restaurant in London, and it was not a good experience. Write a letter to the restaurant and <u>complain</u> about:
> - the food
> - the service
> - other guests
>
> <u>Include:</u>
> what you expect the restaurant to do
>
> Find a suitable beginning and ending. **Write about 200 words.**

Schritt 5: Überprüfe jetzt deinen Text.
Dafür kannst du diese Checkliste verwenden.

Checkliste:	
Mein Text hat die geforderte Länge (mindestens 200 Wörter).	☐
Ich habe einen passenden Anfang und Schluss geschrieben.	☐
Task achievement: Ich habe alle vier Aspekte berücksichtigt und ausgearbeitet.	☐
Coherence&cohesion: Mein Text enthält eine Bandbreite an sinnvollen Verbindungswörtern.	☐
Grammar: Mein Text enthält eine Vielfalt an (auch komplexeren) grammatischen Strukturen.	☐
Vocabulary: Ich habe einen angemessenen und breiten Wortschatz verwendet und meine Rechtschreibung überprüft.	☐
Impression of general quality: Der Stil meines Schreibens passt zum Leser und zum Ziel, mich zu beschweren.	☐

Beispiel 2: Bewerbungsschreiben

Bewerbungsschreiben sind ein Spezialfall. Hier gibt es neben der angemessenen Anrede und Grußformel weitere Dinge zu beachten. Deine Bewerbung muss zum Arbeitgeber und zu der Position passen. Es muss deutlich werden, für welchen Job du dich bewirbst und wo du die Anzeige gesehen hast, warum dich dieser Job reizt und welche Qualifikation du dafür mitbringst. Oft werden dir die vier Aspekte *(prompts)* der Aufgabenstellung diese Dinge bereits vorgeben.

You saw an online advert for an assistant to help in a cafe in Brighton during the summer.

Write a **letter of application** and include:
- your reasons for applying
- valuable experience in a previous job
- your personal qualities
- questions about the work

Find a suitable beginning and ending. **Write about 200 words.**

Schritt 1: Lies das Lösungsbeispiel und fülle die Lücken mit Wörtern aus dem Kasten auf der Seite 56.

Dear Sir or Madam

I read your [＿＿＿＿] online and I would like to [＿＿＿＿] for the job of

assistant to help in your cafe this summer.

I would love to work in a cafe because I really enjoy having contact with people. What's more,

English is my favourite lesson at school, and a summer job in your cafe would give me the chance

to [＿＿＿＿] my English.

As you will see from my [＿＿＿＿], I already have some [＿＿＿＿]

because last year I worked in a cafe in Munich. After working in the kitchen for one week, I was

given work with the [＿＿＿＿]. My responsibilities [＿＿＿＿] taking

orders, serving customers and clearing the tables. As a result, I am sure that I have the

[＿＿＿＿] that I will need in your cafe.

As far as my personal qualities are [＿＿＿＿], I am honest, [＿＿＿＿]

and hard-working. I love the interaction with people, but on the other [＿＿＿＿]

I know that the time for talking is limited.

May I please ask you what the [＿＿＿＿] is and whether there is the possibility

of [＿＿＿＿] at the cafe? Also, I can only start as from the 1st July. Is this

[＿＿＿＿] to you?

I look [ ] to hearing from you soon.

Yours [ ],

Daniel Holzberg

acceptable • accommodation • advert • apply • concerned • customers • CV • experience • faithfully • forward • hand • improve • included • pay rate • reliable • skills

Schritt 2: Brauchst du noch etwas Übung mit dem typischen Wortschatz für Bewerbungsschreiben? Ergänze die folgenden Networks.

Tipp

Natürlich darfst du beim Üben und in der Prüfung auch Angaben über Berufserfahrung, Motivation, Kenntnisse etc. erfinden, sie sollten aber realistisch sein und müssen natürlich zum Job passen.

honest

personal qualities

reliable

assistant

work experience

CV

application words

advert

Schritt 3: Jetzt bist du dran. Lies die Aufgabe und schreibe deine Mail.

It's the year 2070 and you want to work as a volunteer during your summer holidays. You see the following advert on the internet:

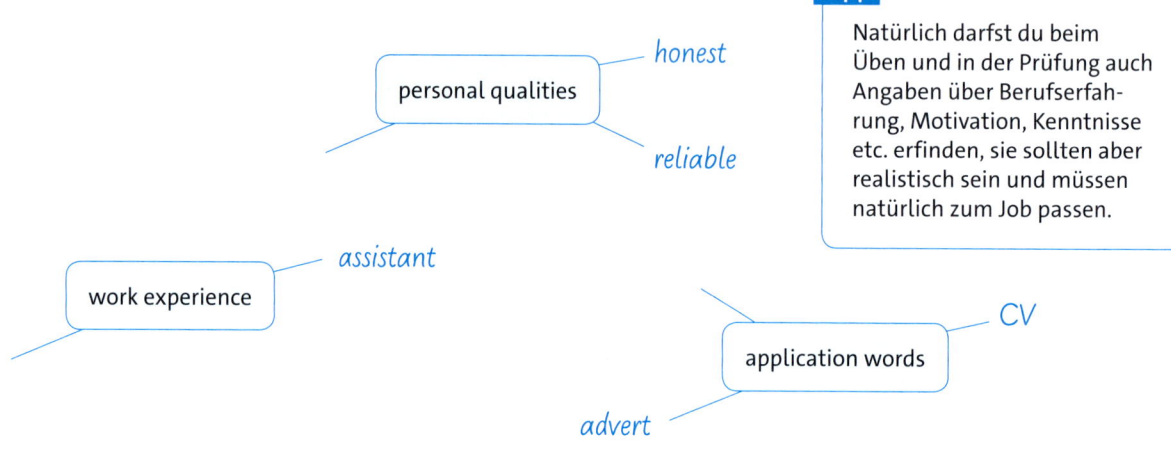

We have volunteer opportunities to suit everyone's skills. It takes a lot of different characters to run a busy robot rescue centre! As a member of our team you will be expected to take part in all the daily tasks, which include:

• feeding robot babies
• cleaning out shelters and pools
• observing and counting robots
• assisting our experts
• showing school groups around

Please send your application to manager@robot-rescuers.com

Write an **email of application** and include:
• your reason for applying
• valuable experience for the job
• your personal qualities
• questions about the work

Find a suitable beginning and ending. **Write about 200 words.**

Schritt 4: Überprüfe jetzt deinen Text.
Dafür kannst du diese Checkliste verwenden:

Checkliste:	
Mein Text hat die geforderte Länge (mindestens 200 Wörter).	☐
Ich habe einen passenden Anfang und Schluss geschrieben.	☐
Task achievement: Ich habe alle vier Aspekte berücksichtigt und ausgearbeitet.	☐
Coherence&cohesion: Mein Text enthält eine Bandbreite an sinnvollen Verbindungswörtern.	☐
Grammar: Mein Text enthält eine Vielfalt an (auch komplexeren) grammatischen Strukturen.	☐
Vocabulary: Ich habe einen angemessenen und breiten Wortschatz verwendet und meine Rechtschreibung überprüft.	☐
Impression of general quality: Der Stil meines Schreibens passt zum Leser und zum Ziel, mich zu bewerben.	☐

Articles

Ein weiteres Aufgabenformat beim *Guided Writing* ist das Verfassen eines Artikels, z.B. für eine Schulzeitung oder -Website. Es wird dir ein Thema gegeben, über das du mit Hilfe von vier Aspekten berichten sollst. Dies kann ein vergangenes Ereignis sein (z.B. ein Schulausflug), ein Bericht über ein aktuelles Ereignis (z.B. die Aktivitäten eines Schulklubs) oder ein zukünftiges Thema (z. B. Pläne für ein neues Schulcafé). Es kann auch eine Meinungsäußerung von dir verlangt werden.

Ein Artikel ist meist in einer sachlich-informativen Sprache verfasst – auch bei Meinungsäußerungen. Denke aber auch daran, wo dein Artikel erscheint und wer ihn lesen wird. Sind Gleichaltrige deine Zielgruppe, so kann der Ton natürlich lockerer sein, als wenn du ein breiteres Publikum oder Erwachsene ansprichst.

> **Tipp**
>
> Keine Panik, wenn du zu einem Thema keine eigene Erfahrung hast. Hier ist bloß Fantasie gefragt – du darfst alles frei erfinden.

Die Prüfungsaufgabe kann zum Beispiel so aussehen:

> Last year some students from your class spent a week in a school in Britain. Now 15 students from the British school are going to spend a week in your school. Write an **article** about the coming visit for your school magazine.
>
> In your article include the following aspects:
> *   highlights of last year's visit to Britain
> *   programme for the British students
> *   accommodation for the British students
> *   a call for readers to help with the visit
>
> **Write about 200 words.**

Schritt 1: Mache dir Notizen. Beachte dabei die von dir verlangte Struktur (vier Aspekte).

		mentioned	included	elaborated	fully elaborated
1	highlights last year				
2	programme				
3	accommodation				
4	call for help				

Schritt 2: Schreibe nun deinen Text. Verwende dabei deine Notizen. Die Reihenfolge, in der du die vier Aspekte abarbeitest, spielt keine Rolle.

Denke neben dem Inhalt auch an die anderen, gleich wichtigen Bewertungskriterien:
- Strukturiere deinen Text durch Verbindungswörter. Nutze dafür auch die Übersicht auf Seite 50.
- Achte bei deinen grammatischen Strukturen auf Vielfalt und Korrektheit.
- Verwende einen breiten und angemessenen Wortschatz und denk an die Rechtschreibung.

Tipp

Verbessere deinen Text!

Verbindungswörter	Grammatik	Wortschatz
Verbindungswörter kann man manchmal auch noch ganz gut im Nachhinein einbauen, z.B.: *We had lessons and went on trips to places near York.* → *We not only had lessons, but also went on trips to places near York.*	Auch bei der Grammatik kannst du vor der Reinschrift noch nachbessern, z.B.: *In May last year 15 lucky students spent a week in York. I was one of them.* → *In May last year I was one of 15 lucky students who spent a week in York.*	Nutze deine Chance, den verwendeten Wortschatz aufzupolieren, z.B.: *We found families ...* → *We managed to find families ...* *We'll be happy to hear from you.* → *We'll be delighted to hear from you.*

Schritt 3: Überprüfe jetzt deinen Text. Dafür kannst du die Checkliste von Seite 50 verwenden.

Blogs

Da es sich um einen persönlichen Text handelt, ist beim Verfassen eines Blogs eine gewisse Stilfreiheit erlaubt. Du bekommst aber wie bei allen anderen Aufgabenformaten in *Guided Writing* vier Aspekte, die du erwähnen und ausarbeiten solltest. Oft sind auch ein oder zwei Anfangssätze vorgegeben.

Die Prüfungsaufgabe kann zum Beispiel so aussehen:

> You are on a tour of Europe with a good friend. Every few days you write a blog entry about your adventures. Now, on the evening before the last day of the journey, you write your final blog entry.
>
> In your **blog entry** include the following aspects:
> - what you did today
> - your best experience(s) on the journey
> - what you have learned from the journey
> - your feelings about the last day
>
> Your blog entry starts like this:
>
> > Hi guys!
> > This is my final blog – I can't really believe it! We've had another great day today: ...
>
> Continue the blog. **Write about 200 words.**

Schritt 1: Mache dir Notizen. Beachte dabei die von dir verlangte Struktur (vier Aspekte).

	mentioned	included	elaborated	fully elaborated
1	*what you did today*			
2				
3				
4				

Schritt 2: Schreibe nun deinen Text. Verwende dabei deine Notizen. Denke auch an die anderen drei Bewertungskriterien.

> **Tipp**
>
> In Blogs verwendet man oft eine emotionale, subjektive Sprache, z. B. wenn man beschreibt, was einem gefallen oder gar nicht gefallen hat. Dafür ist es gut, wenn du viele verschiedene aussagekräftige Adjektive kennst. Sammele Alternativen für *nice* und *not nice*.
>
> - statt: *Rome was nice.: Rome was fantastic, special, ...*
> - statt: *Rome wasn't nice.: Rome was disappointing, awful, ...*

> **Tipp**
>
> In einem Blog hast du mehr sprachliche Freiheiten, z.B. sind in einem Blog auch (gekonnt eingesetzte) unvollständige Sätze erlaubt, z.B.
>
> *There were many young people, and there was such great music!*
>
> → *So many young people, and such great music!*

Schritt 3: Überprüfe jetzt deinen Text. Dafür kannst du die Checkliste von Seite 50 verwenden.

Stories

Bei diesem Aufgabenformat schreibst du anhand einer vorgegebenen Situation sowie der üblichen vier Aspekte eine frei erfundene Geschichte.

Tipp

Was ist bei Geschichten zu beachten?
- Geschichten kannst du aus verschiedenen **Perspektiven** schreiben (Ich-Erzähler oder 3. Person). Wenn du dich entschieden hast, musst du bei dieser Perspektive bleiben.
- Geschichten werden meist in der **Vergangenheit** erzählt. Verwende also für die Haupthandlung das *simple past*. Wiederhole das *simple past* mithilfe der interaktiven Übungen auf www.scook.de.
- **Wörtliche Rede**, **Fragen** und treffende **Adjektive** machen deine Geschichte lebendiger.
- Geschichten haben einen **Spannungsbogen**:
  - Schauplatz, Zeit, Personen etc. werden vorgestellt (Ausgangssituation).
  - Dann passiert etwas Überraschendes/Wunderbares/Schreckliches (Höhe- oder Wendepunkt).
  - Das führt zu einer neuen Situation (Auflösung eines Rätsels, Happy End, etc.).

Die Prüfungsaufgabe kann zum Beispiel so aussehen:

You take part in an international story writing competition. All the stories in the competition have to be written in English.

Write a **story** and include the following aspects:
- a day at work
- a surprise
- a problem
- a happy ending

Find a suitable beginning and ending. **Write about 200 words.**

Schritt 1: Mache dir Notizen. Beachte dabei die von dir verlangte Struktur (vier Aspekte).

	mentioned	included	elaborated	fully elaborated
1	*a day at work*			
2				
3				
4				

Schritt 2: Schreibe nun deinen Text. Verwende dabei deine Notizen. Denke auch an die anderen drei Bewertungskriterien.

Tipp

Eine Geschichte bewegt sich nach vorne. Sammle daher in den Wochen vor der Prüfung *linking phrases* und *time adverbials:* then, after that, suddenly, …

Sammle auch aussagekräftige **Adjektive**: *person:* calm, nervous, silly, serious, …
        feelings: happy, sad, jealous, proud, …

Schritt 3: Überprüfe jetzt deinen Text. Dafür kannst du die Checkliste von Seite 50 verwenden.

ABSCHLUSS-
PRÜFUNGS-
TRAINER

Realschulabschluss
Bayern

Musterprüfungen

MUSTERPRÜFUNG 1: Written Test (Time: 105 minutes)

City life in Britain
PART I: Reading

High-rise living in Britain

High-rise apartment blocks have long had a bad press in Britain. People think of the tower blocks that were built in the 1960s for people in lower-paid jobs. The flats were small, the entrances dark and dirty, and full of litter and graffiti. The lifts kept breaking down. That was no joke if you lived on the 10th floor and arrived home with your week's shopping and a child in a pushchair. **(1)**

Of course, the tower blocks have always had their fans, above all because of the amazing views from the higher flats. The residents of tower blocks also often say that they feel safer than in a house. After all, nobody can climb through the window of a flat on the 16th floor. **(2)** In fact, nobody can even look in, so you don't have to draw your curtains at night. And the flats are largely free from mice, ants and spiders.

The voices in favour of tower blocks were long in the minority. But not any more. Look at the skyline of most British cities today and you'll see that apartment blocks are going up all around you. **(3)** Why this sudden popularity of flats? One reason is that with land becoming more and more expensive, houses are becoming unaffordable. Building taller, it seems, is the only way of building cheaper homes. Some of these modern flats are built as 'pods' – that is to say, each flat is built as a self-contained unit, with bathrooms and kitchen that are equipped to a high standard, and the pods are then simply placed one on top of the other. **(4)** This is often less costly than traditional building techniques, and customers can make their choice of equipment as they would do if they were purchasing a car.

It is true that families with children still usually prefer to live in a house with a front door, a back door and a garden. But these days there are more childless couples and people who live on their own. **(5)** They often get home from work late and don't want the bother of garden work. Instead, they prefer to have a few plants on an easily-managed balcony. This ex-

Tower block in London

plains why the apartments going up today are built to attract people on good incomes. The flats are large and airy. CCTV cameras keep the entrances safe. **(6)** And companies are employed to clean the corridors and maintain the lifts.

What's more, a recent report has challenged the widely-held view that high-rise blocks offer a less healthy environment. **(7)** Experts from the University of Bern in Switzerland found that people who live on the 8th floor or above are likely to live longer than those who live on the lower floors. Those living higher up, they claim, are 40% less likely to die of lung disease, and 35% less likely to die from heart disease. That's because walking up more stairs keeps people fitter. There is less air pollution on the higher floors and moreover people are less affected by traffic noise. **(8)**

The British population is expected to grow from about 65 million in 2016 to 75 million by 2040. So there will be a need for millions of new homes. If we want to protect our countryside, we will have to build them in our cities. But we all know that land in cities is costly, too costly for millions of new houses. **(9)** In other words, in future more people will have to live in flats. The apartment blocks being built today are here to stay.

TASK 1: Read the text *High-rise living in Britain*. Are sentences 1–6 *True* (T) or *False* (F)? If there is not enough information to answer *True* or *False*, choose *Not in the text* (N). **Tick (✓) the correct answer.**

		T	F	N
1	The 1960s tower blocks were often in poor condition.	☐	☐	☐
2	One advantage of flats is that they attract fewer harmful animals than houses.	☐	☐	☐
3	Flats used to be very popular, but nowadays most people want to live in houses.	☐	☐	☐
4	Pods are cheap, but people prefer to live in flats with individual characteristics.	☐	☐	☐
5	Today fewer people want to do garden work.	☐	☐	☐
6	The housing problem will solve itself because fewer people will live in Britain in the future.	☐	☐	☐

_____ / 6

TASK 2: Look at the text *High-rise living in Britain*. Six sentences have been removed from the text. Choose the correct gap (1–9) in the text for each of the sentences below (A–F). **Write the correct number of the gap behind each sentence.** Be careful, there are **three gaps** that you **do not need to use**.

A	And there are more people who live in one town and work in another.	☐
B	So even without garden work people live healthier lives.	☐
C	The general opinion was that people only lived in such buildings if they had no alternative.	☐
D	The only solution then is to enable more people to live on each small plot of land.	☐
E	Reception areas are light and welcoming.	☐
F	The sky is thick with cranes.	☐

_____ / 6

> **TASK 3:** Read the article about youth orchestras in Manchester and look carefully at each line. Some lines are correct, but **six** of the lines 1–15 have a word which should not be there. **Write the words which should not be there on the lines next to the text.** There is one example **(0)** at the beginning.

Six Youth Orchestras in Manchester

0	The Manchester Youth Orchestras are open to all of young musicians	*of*
1	and cater for all musical levels: we have six different orchestras,	
2	meaning that players of all abilities have an opportunity when to make	
3	music with people who are of much the same ability as they are.	
4	As our orchestras meet on Saturday mornings and additionally on three	
5	days of the week in the school holidays. We are indeed fortunate to be	
6	able to make use of great facilities at the University of Manchester.	
7	We have an excellent team of professional musicians who lead for the	
8	sessions and conduct to a very high standard.	
9	Sessions last the three hours and students pay £50 for each session.	
10	However, we are keen to make music possible for as many young	
11	musicians as are possible and therefore offer some assistance with	
12	course fees to families facing financial difficulties. Make sure that	
13	you apply for this help in the appropriate section of the application form.	
14	Applications are dealt with on a first-come, first-served basis, so do have	
15	apply as early as possible.	

_____ / 6

TASK 4: Look at the following info boxes about places to visit in the city of Birmingham. Match questions 1–6 with the correct places (A–D). **Fill in the correct letter in each box**. The places may be chosen more than once. There is one example **(0)** at the beginning.

A Soho House is the elegant home of Matthew Boulton, a key figure in England's industrial revolution. Boulton, who lived in Soho House from 1766 to 1809, is famous for building, with James Watt, the world's most efficient steam engines at that date, and his home had a steam heated bath and one of the first central heating systems in England since the time of the Romans! Another innovation were the indoor toilets cleaned with running water. You can admire these technological wonders in addition to the elegant furniture and decorations of the reception and bedrooms. And following your visit through the rooms, you can see an exhibition of coins, buttons, clocks, vases and other products that Boulton made in a nearby factory.

B Sarehole Mill stands in the countryside only a few miles from Birmingham city centre. A mill has stood here since 1542, but the building we see today was built in 1771. It was used from 1756 to 1761 by Matthew Boulton as a 'flatting mill', i.e. to make the metal that Boulton needed to manufacture his products. The mill was working till 1919; after that it was disused for many years. It was saved from demolition by local campaigners and the mill was finally restored in 1969. It still has two waterwheels, and one of them is in operation every Wednesday and Sunday to grind corn that visitors may purchase in the mill shop.

C Back-to-back houses were built during England's industrial revolution and were the lowest standard of housing provided for factory workers. Sharing a wall with neighbouring houses on three of their four sides, i.e. to both sides and to the back, they only had a door and windows to the front. As a result, they were badly ventilated and damp. They had no central heating, but relied instead on open fires that often filled the rooms with smoke. Nearly half the population of Birmingham lived in houses like this during the 19th century. Most have now been demolished, but the Back to Backs run by the National Trust in Birmingham give you a rare chance to see this important part of England's industrial past.

D Birmingham's Black Country Living Museum is packed with evidence of the city's industrial past. Look around the houses of miners, then enter deep into an underground mine to see the inhuman conditions in which the miners worked. Admire a full-scale working replica of the very first working steam engine in the world – the Newcomen engine of 1712. Then visit shops, e.g. a sweet shop and chemist's, that look just as they did in the early 19th century. Wherever you go, guides in historic costumes can explain what you are seeing and bring Birmingham's industrial past back to life.

Which of the places ...

0	has a shop where you can buy things?	B
1	has a copy of the world's first steam engine?	
2	is the place where Matthew Boulton produced the metal for his coins, buttons and clocks?	
3	shows you some of the worst houses ever built in Britain?	
4	has beautiful old tables, beds and chests of drawers?	
5	was almost destroyed?	
6	has a primitive heating system?	

_____ / 6

TASK 5: Verwende die Informationen aus einem Reiseführer über eine besondere Attraktion in London. **Bearbeite die Aufgaben (1–5) stichpunktartig auf Deutsch.** Es ist keine wörtliche Übersetzung nötig, die Aspekte müssen <u>inhaltlich</u> jedoch <u>vollständig</u> erfasst sein. Einzelwörter genügen nicht als Antwort.

The Mousetrap, a murder mystery play by Agatha Christie, has been performed in London six days a week for 60 years, easily making it the longest-running play in the world. It has been running so long, in fact, that around 400 different actors have acted in it over the years. One actress, Natasha Rickman, played the very same role that her mother had played many years before!

Agatha Christie actually wrote *The Mousetrap* as a radio play in 1947. But when it was first performed on stage, most theatre critics were not impressed. Agatha Christie herself predicted that it would run for a maximum of eight months. But the theatre-goers proved them all wrong.

Of course, being a murder mystery, everybody wants to know who commits the crime: that, after all, is the point of the play. So given that nearly eleven million people have watched the play, you might have thought the secret would by now be common knowledge. But at the end of every show, the members of the audience are asked not to reveal the secret or to share it on the social media. And the impressive thing is that by and large the secret has been kept. Agatha Christie herself helped to keep the secret by making sure that the play has not been published as a book in the UK, and the play has never been made into a film.

1   In welcher Hinsicht hat *The Mousetrap* einen Weltrekord aufgestellt?

_____ 1

2   Was war das Besondere, als Natasha Rickman eine Rolle übernahm?

_____ 1

3   Wie unterschied sich die Reaktion des Publikums von der Reaktion der Theaterkritiker?

_____ 1

4   Welche Erwartungen hatte Agatha Christie selbst an das Stück?

_____ 1

5   Wie wurde es erreicht, dass die Auflösung des Verbrechens bis heute nicht verraten wird? **(2 Aspekte)**

_____

_____ 2

_____ / 6

PART II: Use of English

> **TASK 1:** Look at the text on page 62. **Find a word or expression which means <u>the same as</u> each of the words (1−5) below.** The lines where you can find the words or expressions are indicated in brackets. There is one example **(0)** at the beginning.

0	(to) construct	→	*built / (to) build*	(l. 1−9)
1	(a) hall	→		(l. 1−9)
2	rubbish	→		(l. 1−9)
3	naturally	→		(l. 10−18)
4	(to) lay	→		(l. 19−36)
5	alone	→		(l. 37−49)

_____ / 5

> **TASK 2:** Look at the text on page 62. What do the following words mean? **Match** the expressions (A−F) **<u>as used in the text</u>** with their corresponding definitions (0−7). **Write the correct numbers in the grid below.** Be careful: There are two definitions that you do not need. One definition **(0)** has already been matched correctly.

A	**to break down** (l. 6)	**0**	**to stop working**
B	to equip (l. 30)	**1**	to steal
C	to purchase (l. 35)	**2**	to provide with facilities
D	to attract (l. 46)	**3**	to change the colour of something
E	to maintain (l. 49)	**4**	to keep in good condition
F	to protect (l. 66)	**5**	to keep safe from damage
		6	to catch the attention of somebody
		7	to buy

A	B	C	D	E	F
0					

_____ / 5

TASK 3: Use the word given in capitals at the end of some of the lines to **form a word of the same word family** that fits in the space in the same line. There is one example **(0)** at the beginning.

Part-time job opportunity in Sheffield

0	The Sheffield Parks Division needs *helpers* for the current	**HELP**
	restoration of three Victorian parks across the city. Your task	
1	will be to assist our team of _____	**PROFESSOR**
	park keepers. Most of your work will be carried out outside.	
2	It will involve _____ trees and flowers,	**PLANT**
3	repairing _____ fences and similar tasks. These	**BREAK**
4	part-time jobs, which are _____ at a rate of £8.50 an hour,	**PAY**
5	will be _____ from the beginning of May.	**AVAILABILITY**
	Please send us your CV and the names of two people who can	
6	write you a _____.	**REFER**

_____ / 6

TASK 4: Complete the second sentence so that it has a similar meaning to the first sentence, using the KEY WORD given in brackets. **Do not change the KEY WORD given. You must use between two and five words including the KEY WORD.** There is one example **(0)** at the beginning.

0 Research shows that the aim of most adults in Britain is to get a job.   **(WANT)**

Research shows that most adults in Britain *want to* get a job.

1 Of course not everyone is able to gain employment.   **(SUCCEEDS)**

Of course not everyone _____ employment.

2 But most people understand the advantages of being in work.   **(BY)**

But the advantages of being in work _____ most people.

3 Employment not only provides an income but also a greater sense of self-value.   **(AS)**

Employment provides an income _____ a greater sense of self-value.

4 And most people want to leave the house. They don't want to stay at home all day.   **(INSTEAD)**

And most people want to leave the house _____ at home all day.

_____ / 4

TASK 5: Complete the following text. Use the correct forms of the words in brackets and find words of your own to replace the question marks. There is one example **(0)** at the beginning.

My fear of going abroad

I was never any good at **(0)** _learning_ **(learn)** foreign languages. I started with German in

Year 7, but I could never understand why **(1)** _____ **(???)** were so many different

words that all meant *the*. Then in Year 8 we had French as our second foreign language,

and that was even **(2)** _____ **(difficult)**. I never enjoyed the lessons

and my marks were **(3)** _____ **(spectacular)** awful.

My sad experience with foreign languages at school made me nervous about **(4)** _____

(travel) abroad. How, I thought, could I tell a hotel receptionist that I **(5)** _____

(need) a toothbrush? Or how could I understand what I **(6)** _____ **(tell)** by

a foreign police officer? It seemed **(7)** _____ **(???)** a nightmare.

So when Phil, my **(8)** _____ **(good)** friend at school, suggested a cycling holiday

in France, my immediate reply **(9)** _____ **(can imagine)**.

I of **(10)** _____ **(???)** said "No".

_____ / 10

PART III: Guided Writing

You only have to do <u>one</u> of the following two tasks.
Important: First read both tasks, then decide whether you want to do Task A or Task B.

You can write down your ideas on your extra sheet before you do the task on your exam paper.

TASK A:

Imagine you are living in the year 2125. You are writing the first **blog entry** for your new Cyber Blog.
Include information about:
- your home
- your daily life
- your weekend activities
- a problem that you had this week and how you solved it.

Find a suitable beginning and ending. **Write about 200 words.**

TASK B:

You want to spend part of the summer in London and you have found a Day Centre for old people that requires assistant helpers. The work involves serving tea and snacks, chatting with the old people, and helping them with their shopping.

Write a **letter of application** to the Day Centre. Include the following aspects:
- your reasons for applying
- valuable experience with previous jobs
- personal qualifications
- questions about the work.

Find a suitable beginning and ending. **Write about 200 words.**

_____ / 30

Listening Test (Time: 30 minutes)

TASK 1: You will hear five people. What is their reason for speaking? **Write the correct numbers (1–5) in the boxes next to the categories (A–H).** Be careful: Use each number only once.
(You will have 5 seconds after the first listening and 5 seconds after the second listening.)

A Offering employment	☐	**E** Describing a new game	☐
B Asking for information	☐	**F** Giving directions	☐
C Changing the date of treatment	☐	**G** Recommending healthy food	☐
D Advertising a tourist site	☐	**H** Campaigning for road safety	☐

_____ / 5

10

TASK 2: You will hear an interview with Paul Finnegan, an English teenager who travelled to France with his friend Phil. One ending to each of the following sentences (1–4) is correct. **Tick (✓) A, B, C or D.** (You will have 5 seconds after the first listening and 5 seconds after the second listening.)

1 Paul Finnegan says that …

   A ☐ he joked during language lessons at school.

   B ☐ he has good memories of his language lessons at school.

   C ☐ his language lessons prepared him well for travelling abroad.

   D ☐ his language lessons taught him little.

2 On the way to the hostel in Calais …

   A ☐ Paul felt more confident than he expected.

   B ☐ the boys had an experience that ended well.

   C ☐ everything was so bad that they nearly turned home.

   D ☐ Paul asked his first question in French.

3 In the hostel in Calais …

   A ☐ Paul looked forward to talking with the Serbian boys.

   B ☐ the boy from Serbia communicated by using a dictionary.

   C ☐ Paul was unable to understand the Serbian boy.

   D ☐ the boy from Serbia went on talking until Paul understood.

4 At the end of the evening Paul understood that …

   A ☐ the Serbian boys wanted to come to London.

   B ☐ you have to learn a foreign language if you want to communicate abroad.

   C ☐ you can communicate if you are confident, patient and good-humoured.

   D ☐ what's most important in communicating is the content of the message.

_____ / 4

11

TASK 3: You will hear a report from a famous tourist site in Brighton. **Underline the wrong words in the text and write the correct version in the space provided.**
(You will have 10 seconds after the first listening and 15 seconds after the second listening.)

Hi, I'm standing on the seafront in Brighton. The sun is shining, the beach is _____

dizzy – but the sea ... is cold! Too cold for swimming. That's often the _____

problem here in Brighton, so the town has always provided attractions in _____

order to keep the tourists drumming. And with this latest attraction, the _____

British Airways i360, which opened in August 2016, Brighton hopes to keep _____

its 11 million visitors per year coming well into the future. _____

So what is the British Airways i360? Imagine a narrow concrete tower, _____

162 metres high. You travel up the tower in a large cabin, or capsule, _____

that slides up all around the outside of the tower. 200 people have _____

place in the cabin: they can move around in it, and enjoy a 360-degree _____

view of the town below, with the sea on one side, and the green hills _____

of the Sussex countryside on the other. _____

The i360 was designed by the same architects that designed the famous _____

London Eye, and like in the Eye, you pay to travel slowly up the tower, _____

enjoy the new from the top, and travel slowly back down again. _____

_____ / 5

12

TASK 4: You will hear a radio interview with an Indian cricket expert. **Complete the notes.** You do not have to write complete sentences but **one word is not enough.**
(You will have 10 seconds after the first listening and 20 seconds after the second listening.)

The role of cricket in India			_____ / 8
A comparison between cricket and basketball:	**Cricket:**	**Basketball:**	
Number of countries in the World Cup:			1
Number of fans worldwide:			1
Reasons why cricket has so many fans:			
1)			1
2)			1
What people in other countries know about cricket:			
1)			1
2)			1
New features in Twenty20 Cricket:			
1)			1
2)			1

13

TASK 5: You will hear an interview with Liz and Richard about their visit to the islands of St Kilda. **Listen to the interview and take notes.** Be careful, **one word is not enough**.
(You will have 30 seconds after the first listening and 90 seconds after the second listening.)

1 The position of the islands of St Kilda is special because they are …

_____ 1

2 Liz and Richard went there because they wanted to see …

_____ 1

3 It wasn't easy to get to St Kilda because …

_____ 1

4 What makes the St Kilda mice and sheep so special is that …

_____ 1

5 The St Kildans survived by … _____

and _____ 1

6 The rocks are so steep that the people couldn't keep boats and so they …

_____ 1

7 The population of St Kilda fell because the young left and …

_____ 1

8 On St Kilda today you see a museum and …

_____ 1

_____ / 8

MUSTERPRÜFUNG 2: Written Test (Time: 105 minutes)

South Africa – a fascinating country
PART I: Reading

Life in South Africa today

Society is constantly changing in every country in the world, but few countries have changed as radically as South Africa since the country's first free elections in 1994. Before that, everything in your life depended on the colour of your skin. Under a system called apartheid, black and white people lived in different zones, went to different schools, had different jobs, and relaxed on different beaches. **(1)** Black people could not vote, and marriages between black and white people were forbidden. This system led to street protests by the black population, which were put down violently by the forces of the white government. Many unarmed protesters were killed, many more were locked up in prison. **(2)**

The election of Nelson Mandela, South Africa's first black president, in 1994 changed all that. **(3)**. Diversity and multiculturalism are now celebrated. All South Africans now enjoy equal rights. The country has eleven official languages: English, Afrikaans (a language that derives from Dutch) and nine African languages. The result is that local communities can now send their children to schools which teach in their own language. For its success in all these areas South Africa is often called the Rainbow Nation.

However, improvements are coming too slowly for many black South Africans who were born after 1994. The white population (nine percent of the total population) still has control of more of the country's wealth than black South Africans, who make up 80 percent of the population. **(4)**. But the inescapable truth is that about 54 percent of the black population live in poverty, according to a government report in 2014, compared to 0.8 percent of the white population. You see this inequality in many of South Africa's primary and secondary schools. Schools in mostly white areas of the country are well equipped, while schools in mostly black areas frequently have poor facilities. And we are not only talking here about a lack of computers; more importantly, there may well be only one toilet for 60 students. **(5)** What's more, schools that teach in an African language often find it difficult to employ teachers who can speak their language.

While life is not easy for many black South Africans, it is particularly hard for girls because they suffer most from the violence in the streets. In fact, about one third of girls experience sexual violence before the age of 18. The rates of HIV infections are frighteningly high, and over 60 percent of the victims are women. Many children have to manage life on their own because their parents die young, and they often have to leave school and look after younger brothers and sisters. **(6)** And not surprisingly, the children are often frightened of falling ill themselves.

South Africa's economy is now growing by less than two percent a year, which is a lower increase than in the first years of the 21st century. That is a real problem because the government now has less money to spend on schools and social conditions than it did before. But on the other hand, South Africa's problems should not be exaggerated. The country has not been

70 destroyed by violence, as many forecasters predicted prior to the 1994 elections. The economy is Africa's biggest after Nigeria. **(7).** Conditions have improved for the majority of people, and blacks can visit the same beaches and bars as 75 whites. **(8)** The gap between the standard of living of black and white South Africans is still large, and while it's true that on the whole blacks and whites get on better than before, there's little real mixing of the two different populations. So it's not surprising that many blacks are becoming impatient for real change. 80

TASK 1: Read the text *Life in South Africa today*. Six sentences have been removed from the text. Choose the correct gap (1−8) in the text for each of the sentences below (A−F). **Write the correct number of the gap behind each sentence.** Be careful: There are **two gaps** which you do **not need to use**.

A   So they miss out on their education. ☐

B   However, life is still hard for many South Africans. ☐

C   True, a small number of black people have now become rich. ☐

D   And incomes per person are among the highest in Africa. ☐

E   They even used different public toilets. ☐

F   Apartheid was abolished. ☐

_____ / 6

TASK 2: Read the text *Life in South Africa today*. Are sentences 1−10 *True* (T) or *False* (F)? Choose *Not in the text* (N) if there is not enough information to answer *True* or *False*. **Tick (✓) the correct answer.**

		T	F	N
1	The writer thinks that life in South Africa has changed less than in most countries.	☐	☐	☐
2	Before 1994, black South Africans were not allowed to take part in elections.	☐	☐	☐
3	In the years of apartheid, the police often helped peaceful black protesters.	☐	☐	☐
4	Today, children in South Africa have to learn eleven languages at school.	☐	☐	☐
5	*Rainbow Nation* is a negative name for modern South Africa.	☐	☐	☐
6	Younger South Africans feel that conditions are not changing fast enough.	☐	☐	☐
7	The country's social problems are worse for girls than for boys.	☐	☐	☐
8	Many South African children have to take care of themselves and don't go to school because their parents are dead.	☐	☐	☐
9	Today, South Africans have the biggest economy in Africa.	☐	☐	☐
10	The writer's opinion is that South Africa's economy is going to improve in the future.	☐	☐	☐

_____ / 10

TASK 3: Read the following short passage from a travel guide and look carefully at each line. Some lines are correct, but **seven** of the lines 1–10 have a word which should not be there. If a line is correct, put a tick (✓). If a line has **a word which should not be there, write the word** in the space provided. There are two examples **(0)** at the beginning.

Number 46664

0	The small island off the coast of Cape Town, at the very southern tip	✓
0	of South Africa, goes on by the name of Robben Island. It has a sad	*on*
1	past because it was used as well a prison during the years of	___
2	apartheid. Indeed, this it is where Nelson Mandela was a prisoner	___
3	for seventeen years from 1964. During this time the prison staff	___
4	called at him by his number – 46664. This number meant	___
5	so that he had been the 466th prisoner on Robben Island in 1964.	___
6	Nelson Mandela was of course later released from prison, and later	___
7	still he has became the first elected president of South Africa. But for	___
8	the rest of his life Mandela was still sometimes called Prisoner 46664 –	___
9	not as a term of abuse, but on the contrary as if a sign of enormous	___
10	respect for the long years he had been survived in prison.	___

_____ / 7

TASK 4: Verwende die Informationen aus folgender Broschüre über einen Nationalpark in Südafrika. **Bearbeite die Aufgaben (1–5) stichpunktartig auf Deutsch**. Es ist keine wörtliche Übersetzung nötig, die Aspekte müssen <u>inhaltlich</u> jedoch <u>vollständig</u> erfasst sein. Einzelwörter genügen nicht als Antwort.

Visit the Kruger Park – South Africa's most exciting and spectacular safari park

Kruger Park, which was established in 1898, is enormous. It offers its visitors one of the most diverse variety of animals of any wildlife park in the world. No wonder the park receives more than one and a half million visitors each year!

You can drive through the park in a self-drive safari, in which you bring your own vehicle at your own risk. Alternatively you can join a small number of fellow visitors and accompany rangers on foot or in small pick-up trucks.

Accommodation in the park comes in the form of rest-camps, each of which offers a range of accommodation types to suit every budget – anything from huts and bungalows to fully-equipped guest houses. The larger restcamps also offer facilities such as a shop, a first-aid centre, communal kitchen facilities and a petrol station.

The Kruger Park lies in an area that can be infected by malaria, so all necessary precautions have to be taken. Please note that rangers will check that you have protection when you enter the park. At the park entrance you will also be charged a fee for each day you spend in the park. The income raised in this way supports our extensive conservation programme.

Please observe the Park's regulations at all times, and note that you must obtain an exit permit when you leave the park.

1 Was passiert am Eingang des Parks? **(2 Aspekte)**

_____

_____ 2

2 Auf welche Weise kann man den Park besuchen? **(2 Aspekte)**

_____

_____ 2

3 Was bietet der Park in Bezug auf die Tierwelt?

_____ 1

4 Was bieten die größeren Restcamps außer Unterkunft?

_____ 1

5 Was muss man beachten, wenn man den Park wieder verlassen will?

_____ 1

_____ / 7

PART II: Use of English

> **TASK 1:** Look at the text on page 74 / 75. **Find a word or expression which means <u>the same as</u> each of the words (1−5) below.** The lines where you can find the words or expressions are indicated in brackets. There is one example **(0)** at the beginning.

0 always   →   _constantly_ _____ (l. 1−16)

1 (to) ban   →   _____ (l. 1−16)

2 unavoidable   →   _____ (l. 28−48)

3 often   →   _____ (l. 28−48)

4 most   →   _____ (l. 62−81)

5 (to) get better   →   _____ (l. 62−81)

_____ / 5

TASK 2: The following expressions have various meanings. Which of the meanings given in the dictionary is the one used in the text on page 74/75? **Underline** the best German translation.

put down (l. 13)

v. trans **1.** etw. hinlegen **2.** jd. ins Bett bringen *It's time to put the baby down for her sleep.* **3.** töten, einschläfern *(animals)* **4.** etw. aufschreiben *I put down some of my ideas on paper.* **5.** etw. zuschreiben *I put it down to the exercise I've taken recently.* **6.** jd./etw. mies machen **7.** unterdrücken, niederschlagen *(a riot)*

make up (l. 33)

v. trans **1.** etw. erfinden, ausdenken **2.** erstellen *(a list)* **3.** etw. ausmachen, bilden *Women make up 53% of the population.* **4.** kompensieren, ausgleichen *(time) Many employees try to make up hours lost to sickness.* **5.** etw. ergänzen, aufstocken *My son made £170 in his boot sale, so I gave him £30 and made it up to £200.*
v. intr **1.** *(with so.)* sich (mit jd.) vertragen **2.** *(apply cosmetics etc.)* sich schminken

get on (l. 78)

v. trans **1.** anziehen *(shoes, clothes)* **2.** einsteigen in *(train)*
v. intr **1.** Fortschritte machen, vorankommen *I'm getting on well with my trumpet lessons.* **2.** spät werden *Time is getting on, so I'd better go home now.* **3.** auskommen *(agree or live sociably)* **4.** weggehen *I must be getting on now. See you tomorrow!*

_____ / 3

TASK 3: Use the word given in capitals at the end of some of the lines to **form a word of the same word family** that fits in the space in the same line. There is one example **(0)** at the beginning.

A shortage of rain in Cape Town

0 From 2014 Cape Town suffered three years of very low _*rainfall*_____ **RAIN**

1 and early in 2018 the city's water supplies were _____ **DANGEROUS**

2 low. This was despite a _____ in water consumption of **REDUCE**

3 over 60%, according to _____ figures. In February the **GOVERN**

city council had to impose a limit of 50 litres per day on its long-suffering

4 _____ (UK consumers use 150 litres a day). **CITY**

5 If this target could not be _____, said the council, people **ACHIEVEMENT**

6 would have to fetch water at communal pumps. _____, rainy **LUCK**

7 weather in April solved the immediate crisis, but _____ **POLITICS**

are warning that problems remain in the longer term.

_____ / 7

TASK 4: Complete the second sentence so that it has a similar meaning to the first sentence, using the KEY WORD given in brackets. **Do not change the KEY WORD given.** You must use **between two and five words including the KEY WORD.** There is one example **(0)** at the beginning.

Elon Musk, businessman and entrepreneur

0 Elon Musk's place of birth is Pretoria, South Africa.   **(BORN)**

Elon Musk _was born in_____ Pretoria, South Africa.

1 Elon Musk is one of the most famous South Africans today.   **(AS)**

Not many South Africans today are _____ Elon Musk.

2 Elon Musk invests not only in rockets but also in electric cars.   **(BOTH)**

Elon Musk invests _____ electric cars.

3 It was Elon Musk who made electric cars popular.   **(BY)**

Electric cars _____ Elon Musk.

4 Not wanting to increase global warming, Elon Musk helped to develop electric cars.   **(BECAUSE)**

Elon Musk helped to develop electric cars _____
to increase global warming.

5 The realisation of his dreams will affect how we live, too.   **(IF)**

_____ , he will affect how we live, too.

_____ / 5

TASK 5: Complete the following text. Use the correct forms of the words in brackets and find words of your own to replace the question marks. There are two examples **(0)** at the beginning.

Tourism in South Africa

According **(0)** _to_____ **(???)** official figures, South Africa **(0)** _receives_____ **(receive)** about three

and a half million travellers each year. Many of **(1)** _____ **(this)** visitors are from

neighbouring countries such as Zimbabwe. The overseas countries with the **(2)** _____

(large) number of tourists to South Africa are the UK, the USA and Germany. Many tourists come

(3) _____ **(???)** English-speaking countries. They choose South Africa as their holiday

destination because English **(4)** _____ **(speak)** in many parts of South Africa as

a first, second or even **(5)** _____ **(three)** language.

Tourists (6) _____ (???) are primarily attracted by the spectacular scenery discover a rich

cultural heritage, not to mention the amazing variety of wild animals (7) _____ (find)

in the country's many national parks. More (8) _____ (surprising), perhaps,

a large number of tourists come to taste South African wines. Some of the country's earliest vines

(9) _____ (plant) in the 17th century. South African wine is now

exported all (10) _____ (???) the world.

_____ / 10

PART III: Guided Writing

You only have to do <u>one</u> of the following two tasks.
Important: First read both tasks, then decide whether you want to do Task A or Task B.

You can write down your ideas on your extra sheet before you do the task on your exam paper.

TASK A:
You take part in a competition titled **My dream country**. For the competition, you have to write about the country that you would most like to visit.

Write an article for the competition and include information about:
- the country you would most like to visit
- a place that you would like to visit there
- an activity that you would like to do there
- why it is likely (or unlikely) that you will ever visit the country in reality.

Write about 200 words.

TASK B:
During a holiday to South Africa, you stayed in a hotel in Cape Town. Unfortunately, you were very disappointed by the hotel. It was not as decribed in the online advert.

You **write a letter of complaint** to the hotel.
In your letter, describe:
- what you expected from the hotel
- what was wrong with the hotel
- how you were disappointed by the hotel staff
- what you want from the hotel now.

Find a suitable beginning and ending. **Write about 200 words.**

_____ / 30

Listening Test (Time: 30 minutes)

TASK 1: You will hear five Canadians. What is their job? **Write the correct numbers (1–5) in the boxes next to the categories (A–H).** Be careful: Use each number only once.
(You will have 5 seconds after the first listening and 5 seconds after the second listening.)

A Speech therapist ☐

B Translator ☐

C Seaman ☐

D Hairdresser ☐

E Dentist ☐

F Camera operator ☐

G Fairground worker ☐

H Carpet fitter ☐

_____ / 5

TASK 2: You will hear an interview with Jason Calrow, a Canadian architect.
One ending to each of the following sentences (1–4) is correct. **Tick (✓) A, B, C or D.**
(You will have 5 seconds after the first listening and 5 seconds after the second listening.)

1 Canada's underground cities …

  A ☐ are over thirty kilometres long.

  B ☐ were built so that people can stay warm.

  C ☐ are only open in winter, when it's very cold.

  D ☐ are called skyways in Calgary.

2 Skyway or skywalk is the name of …

  A ☐ a bridge over the Niagara Falls.

  B ☐ a theatre in Canada with especially comfortable seats.

  C ☐ a tram in Jacksonville, Florida, that travels above the streets.

  D ☐ a high platform in a Canadian amusement park.

3 The Calgary Skyways …

  A ☐ allow you to walk between dozens of buildings without touching the ground.

  B ☐ are fifteen metres up in the air.

  C ☐ are used by a disappointingly small number of people.

  D ☐ have brought life back to the streets of downtown Calgary.

4 Harold Hanen …

  A ☐ was the first person to walk through the Calgary Skyways in the early 1970s.

  B ☐ was born in the USA.

  C ☐ developed Calgary's Skyways.

  D ☐ did his studies in Calgary, Canada.

_____ / 4

16

> **TASK 3:** You will hear part of a school presentation about Wales – one of the four countries of the United Kingdom. **Underline the wrong words in the text and write the correct version in the space provided.**
> (You will have 10 seconds after the first listening and 15 seconds after the second listening.)

Most of central Wales is very chilly, and the highest mountains in Wales are higher than any mountain in England. Because the region is so hilly, most of the bigger grounds are on the coast. In the centre there are lots of farms and villages, and sheep and cows everywhere. You'll also find lots of beautiful castles in Wales because when an English king wanted to make Wales part of his kingdom, he built lots of castles to control the Welsh population. Most of these castles are still landing.

But Wales isn't all fields and castles. The south of Wales was once one of the world's biggest producers of coal: it was taken out of the mines here and shipped as far away as Australia. Lots of industries queue around the coal mines, so the population grew too. The south of Wales still has its highest population of all time today – although plenty people have moved away since the coal mines closed. In fact, so many Welsh people have emigrated to Australia that its most-heavily populated state is called Blue South ... Wales!

____ / 6

Caerphilly Castle, Wales

17

TASK 4: You will hear a telephone conversation between two friends about a new cycling race in Britain – the Tour de Yorkshire. **Listen and complete the notes**. You do not have to write complete sentences but **one word is not enough**.
(You will have 10 seconds after the first listening and 20 seconds after the second listening.)

Two fantastic cycle races		
What was special about the 2014 Tour de France:		1
How long does the race take?		
Tour de France:		1
Tour de Yorkshire:		1
How people in Yorkshire reacted to the Tour de France (2 examples):		
– *thousands came to see the race*		
–		1
–		1
The meaning of yellow in the Tour de France:		1
Why some cyclists are surprised by the roads in Yorkshire (2 examples):		
–		1
–		1

_____ / 8

Yellow bicycle on the city walls of York, 2014

18

> **TASK 5:** You will hear an interview with two young hikers on an adventure trip.
> **Listen to the interview and take notes.** Be careful, **one word is not enough**.
> (You will have 30 seconds after the first listening and 90 seconds after the second listening.)

1 Jack slept badly because …

_____ 1

2 The reporter is surprised because Katie …

_____ 1

3 The aim of the D of E Award is to enable young people …

_____ 1

4 The expedition at Silver Level lasts …

_____ and _____ 1

5 Participants are allowed to bring a smartphone, but …

_____ 1

6 When Katie and Jack got lost they …

_____ 1

7 They are now waiting because …

_____ 1

_____ / 7